THE BEGINNER'S GUIDEBOOK TO INVESTING

How to Make Money Investing Today

Mark Gruner

Green Bridge Publishing

FREE GIFT

Thanks for buying my book!

I want to make sure that you have the best chance to succeed and will do everything possible to help you become a great investor!

To show my appreciation, I will send you a FREE BOOK, which includes three chapters to help you out.

To get your FREE book - You can go to the following address:

https://greenbridgeco.com/freeinvestingguide/

DISCLAIMER

The material contained in this book is for instructional purposes only. None of the material is, or should be regarded as advice. Accordingly, no person should rely on any of the contents within this book without first obtaining specific advice from the author and publisher, employees and agents accept no responsibility to any person who acts or relies in any way on any of the material without first obtaining specific advice.

The information within this book is provided on an "as is", "as available" basis without warranties of any kind, express or implied, including, but not limited to, those of TITLE, MERCHANTABILITY, FITNESS FOR A PARTICULAR PURPOSE or NON-INFRINGEMENT or any warranty arising from a course of dealing, usage, or trade practice. No oral advice or written information provided shall create a warranty; nor shall readers of this book

For my wife and family.

"I will tell you how to become rich. Close the doors. Be fearful when others are greedy. Be greedy when others are fearful."

- WARREN BUFFETT

CONTENTS

Title Page

Free Gift

Copyright

Disclaimer

Dedication

Epigraph

Preface

Introduction

Chapter 1 - Business and Money Making 1
Machine

Chapter 2 - Investments Basics   5

Chapter 3 - Time Value of Money   19

Chapter 4 - Setting Goals   34

Chapter 5 - Investments   39

Chapter 6 - ETF Strategy   56

Chapter 7 - Dividend strategy   60

Chapter 8 - Value Investing   64

Chapter 9 - Day Trading Strategies   70

Chapter 10 - Investing for the Beginner   78

Chapter 11 - Mindset   93

Chapter 12 - Don't take Advice from   99
Stockbrokers

Chapter 13 - Terminology   107

Chapter 14 - Interest rates and the Fed   115

Chapter 15 - Automatic Screeners   121

Chapter 16 - Artificial Intelligence and   125
Investing

Chapter 17 - Areas to Watch   130

Thanks!   137

Books In This Series   139

Books By This Author   141

Get in Touch with The Author   143

About The Author   145

PREFACE

The reason that I wrote this book is that I want everyone to be able to benefit from one of the best wealth building machines ever made. This is the stock market. Many people feel that the stock market is only for the wealthy. This is not true. Anyone can benefit and everyone should benefit from the stock market. People may feel that they are not rich enough or do not have enough knowledge to benefit. Both of these are not true. You can benefit from the stock market with as little as $1,000. You only need a little knowledge to succeed. This book will show you how to start making money today. You can have a better return than most long time investors, even wealthy investors.

The tools you need to know and the terminology you need to know will be explained in this book. After reading this book, you will feel comfortable and confident in investing. We will show you how you can achieve better returns than most hedge fund managers. We will cover basic terminologies like price-earnings (PE)` ratio and earnings per share. This will allow you to get a better understanding of how the stock market works and why the stock prices change.

The goal of this book is to make you very comfortable with investing and gain confidence so that you will be able to start your investing career. It is important to start right away. As the old saying goes, the best time to plant a tree was 20 years ago, the next best time to plant a tree is today. Yes, if you had invested in the stocks 20 years ago you would be looking at many quite significant gains. Since you are reading this book, likely, you have not been investing for the past 20 years, but now is the time to do so. The sooner you start the sooner you benefit. Just as the sooner you planted the tree, the sooner you will benefit from the shade that is provided from that tree.

Start Right Away
After reading this book you will be in a position to go to your computer open up an account, also to start a dummy account and start making some transactions. We would recommend you start with a dummy account before you start with real transactions. Then once you have done that we would also recommend that you start opening up your real account, do not put money in yet, but

get it ready. Then, when you can see that you start to make some profits and progress and have a certain ability to make some investments that make sense it is time to do the real thing.

We recommend that once you have finished this book you should be able to start immediately, so there are two options that we will give to you that you can choose. The first option is you try right away and the second option is that you try, six months from now. However, we think it's wise that you start right away but you follow the approach where you invest equal portions per year for the next 10 years this way you won't have to worry about paying a higher price for the entry point in the stock or exchange-traded fund (ETF). The entry point of the stock is the amount you pay to get in, this stock can go up or it can go down.

Beginner Strategies
This book covers many strategies, some are geared for the beginner. The best strategy that has the lowest risk and is the simplest to follow, is perfect for the beginner. The great thing with this strategy is that it also has a great rate of return. This is called the ETF strategy. The goal of this book is that you start with this strategy as soon as possible.

Goals
You do want to write down your goals and make

sure that they are reasonable and achievable.

What is Investing?
Investing is simply the concept of putting a certain amount of money down today and taking much more money years from now. If you have an 8% rate of return and put $1,000 today, then in 30 years that will be worth $15,900 and in 40 years that will be worth $41,100. If you kept this amount in the bank, you would have slightly more than $1,000. This is why it is critical to be investing your surplus money and why you should save so that you can have far more tomorrow.

After reading this book in a few short hours you will be ready to invest. We also recommend that you get in touch with us and you let us know when your investments are and we will give you some feedback on the best possible approach. There is one caveat with the strategy we're giving to you, this strategy would always have worked over the last 50 to 100 years. You would have made money with this strategy no matter what time you started, if you invested equally over 10 years you would make a good return 30 years later. The good return is somewhere between 6 to 12%. There is one caveat, if the whole market collapses and never returns, but this has never occurred before and is not likely to occur within the foreseeable future.

Low Risk & Strong Return

The advantage with our approach is it is very low risk, it is simple and you do not need to spend much time following this approach. Our goal is to be able to have our readers gain access to the investing world without feeling that they do not know what they are doing. This lack of confidence can cost you significantly, I know, I used to lack this confidence and spend the first ten years making all the mistakes that come from not understanding stocks and the stock market.

Avoid Mistakes

I have written this book so that you do not have to make the same mistakes and you can save thousands of dollars by just avoiding my mistakes and follow what works.

INTRODUCTION

I wrote this book to help those who are just starting with investing and don't know where to start.
My goal is to make this as easy as possible for you
to learn and for you to be able to learn as quickly
as possible. With that in mind, I have made this
book purposely as short as possible so that you
can get as much value within the quickest amount
of time.

My second goal is that you will be able to start
investing almost immediately. Depending on how
quickly you can read this book, perhaps in a matter of a few hours and then start your investing
journey right away.

I'm outlining a plan for you that requires very little risk and has worked over the past 50 years and
counting. The goal is to deliver a plan that has a
strong rate of return, around 6% to 12%, is simple to implement, does not take much time, and

is low risk. It sounds like we are promising the world, but we are not. If you follow this plan, you will have great success and beat most investors on the market.

Why doesn't everyone do this? Because, they are not aware, just like I was not aware. Most people are earning 4% to 8%, and they are very pleased with this result. Why fix something if they do not consider it to be broken.

The goal of this book is also to get our readers to get a good understanding of investing and feel much more confident. Investing has a lot to do with confidence, if you are second-guessing your strategies, you will likely not follow them, this is how you can lose. Don't do that.

Investing is not about making money overnight it is about making money over the length of your life so that you can retire comfortably and not have to work for your entire life. It is about getting your hard-earned money to work for you, not for you to work for your money.

Many people hold thousands and tens of thousands and even hundreds of thousands of dollars in their bank account earning extremely low-interest rates most of them are earning less than 1% per year. With this book you can double your portfolio in about eight years. If you start investing early enough you will retire at a much younger age and not be concerned about your finances for the rest of your life.

My goal is to teach you the basic terminologies that you need to be able to speak with your broker or to bypass them altogether and do this online. You must get an understanding of the various strategies that you can use and the one that you should start using right away. The first goal is that you can gain an understanding of the terminology and an understanding of how stockbrokers work. Then, how you can use your first investment to make some money.

By the time you put down this book, you will now be in a position to earn money investing. You will now understand what it means to invest and all the terminologies you need to know such as PE ratios Earnings per Share and what is an ETF. What's an index fund? What is a passive fund vs an active fund? What are the benefits of each? The goal is to take you from beginner to get you into an intermediate state and to get you to gain confidence so that you can make your first investment. By the time you finish reading this book, you will be in a position to earn more than 80% of the investors in the market, in terms of rate of return. They may have been investing for longer and have a larger bank account, but you have the tools to get a better rate of return. Investing is about getting the best rate of return with the lowest amount of risk.

CHAPTER 1 - BUSINESS AND MONEY MAKING MACHINE

"THE BEST TIME TO PLANT A TREE IS TWENTY YEARS AGO, THE NEXT BEST TIME TO PLANT A TREE IS TODAY."

- ANCIENT CHINESE PROVERB

When a business runs well, it basically can be said to turn into a money-making machine. It can take a loan out from the bank and earn more profits on that loan to pay off the debts and interest and create more wealth for their shareholders. It can issue more equity and purchase assets then deliver more revenues at a greater rate than investing in banks or giving a loan and receiving interest.

Benefitting from Money Making Machines

How can the average person benefit from this money-making machine? There are two ways to do this, the first way would be to create your own business. But that is a very risky endeavor, it will take a lot of investment, a lot of time and there will be a lot of risks involved. Most new companies go bankrupt within the first five years. While there is a lot of risks here, there is also a lot of potential rewards. Just because something is risky, it does not mean it should not be done. However, to be guaranteed an income, we will not choose this approach due to the high risks involved.

The other option is investing in the shares of a money-making machine or a business. In other words, purchasing a fraction of that company or a share of that company. If you could purchase a certain fraction or a share of a company, then you would be eligible to share in the profits of that company and thereby benefit from that money-making machine. The added benefit here is that the companies are well-run and therefore they are a lot less risky. Most of the ones that you would invest in would have a history of earnings and have great profit ratios. They would have good growth and a good future. You would be paying a higher price, but you can wait until the price is acceptable to you.

Grow your Investment at High Rates
This way you would put your money in at the rate that the company grows at. Hence, if the company

can grow at 10% per year, by investing in that company, your money will also grow at 10% per year. You must take other factors into account, such as whether you are buying at a high price or a low price. If you buy at a high price, then your returns will be quite a bit less than if you had purchased at a bargain price. You should look for deals and aim to buy when the stocks are at the lower end. This is why you should have a list of stocks that look good.

You want to find stocks that have a good history of growth and where the stock prices are on the rise. You also want to factor in dividends. If we compare two companies where the stock prices have both increased at similar rates but one pays out dividends and one does not, then the one paying dividends will be the better choice.

Set Your Goals

You also want to think about your future. If you are planning on investing in stocks that can fund your future, you would want to ensure that you get some dividend-paying stocks, otherwise, you will be forced to sell shares to pay bills. You may be forced to sell at times when the prices are not ideal. This is something to keep in mind when choosing which stocks to buy.

Everyone can Benefit

The great thing with the stock market is that everyone can benefit from buying shares of these companies, that essentially have turned into money-making machines. You would want to focus on those companies that allow for the strongest growth while factoring in the price. If a company has an earnings per share of $1, then every share would earn $1. If that were to be retained going into the future and also you allow for some growth so that in about ten years it would now be earning $2 per share, this would be a good company to invest in.

This is how people can start earning at the same level as all the people who own shares in companies like Amazon, Berkshire Hathaway, McDonald's, Coke, and many more.

Our goal is that you understand how to achieve this and you also get your hard-earned money into these money-making machines and start benefitting from their profits.

CHAPTER 2 - INVESTMENTS BASICS

"RULE #1: NEVER LOSE MONEY; RULE #2: DON'T
FORGET RULE #1."

- WARREN BUFFET

T his book is written specifically so that the beginner can find the easiest way to start investing in stocks. We will go over all the basics that you need to understand in order for you to be a strong investor and gain the confidence you need to succeed.

The first thing you're going to need to do is to understand the terminology. Investing has a lot of specific terms and it is important that you know what each term means.

For example, what is a stockbroker, this would be a good term to understand, it is basically someone that deals in stocks. If you are the investor and you've got money sitting in your bank account and you would like to purchase a stock or share. You have to have a mechanism to do so. So the first thing you need to do is to have access to a broker. The broker is someone or an entity that can exchange your dollars for stocks. Hence a stockbroker, basically affects the transactions that you request. If you want to buy 100 shares of Coke, you need to go through a stockbroker. There are brokers that give you advice and also manage your portfolio. There are fees associated with these brokers. We recommend, you do not go along with these brokers but rather go for the low-cost broker, who simply affects your trades. We do, however, recommend that you speak with a professional. Try to get this advice for free or for a very low cost.

The mechanism for you to make this transaction would be to first set up an account with the stockbroker or the brokerage house, then you would need to put funds into that account, once you have transferred money to that account, you can then tell the broker or the firm how much stock you would like to purchase. You would need to determine either to buy at the market price or to buy at a fixed price that you determine. The fixed price could be lower than the market price, but you are not guaranteed to make the purchase, only if the shares fall below this price. This is the difference from a limit order and a market order. The limit order sets a price, but is not guaranteed to buy, while the market order is basically guaranteed to buy but not necessarily at the price you wish.

If you buy at the market price then you are subject to slight uptakes. These slight changes in the market price may work for you or they may work against you. For example, if a company XYZ is currently trading at $10 and you say you would like to buy a hundred shares at the market the idea being that you buy 100 shares at $10. When you finalize the trade, your price may be slightly higher or lower. If the shares move to $10.25 now, your hundred shares has a cost of $1,025, but you might also find that the shares drop to $9.75 and this will mean that your 100 shares will cost only $975.

Limit Order
You can also put a limit order which basically says that you will buy it an exact price, no more than $9, the problem here is that the price might never drop to $9. This is a good way to ensure that you pay the price that you are willing to pay and not any more than that. The great thing with the limit order is that you set the price that you're willing to buy at. A good strategy to use is not to put exact

dollars as a limit order so if you wanted to buy the stock at $9 instead of putting a limiter order of $9 you would choose a little more than $9. You may decide to go with $9.05 or even $9.15 but really aiming a little bit higher or slightly lower is the way to go if you really want to purchase the stock at about a price $9. If you think about it many people may choose $9 as this is a nice round figure, so choose something a little different and perhaps a bit higher, so that you are ahead of all those that chose $9.

Shares and Stocks

What is going on when you buy shares of a company or stocks of a company. You are actually buying a piece of that company. If you imagine an apple pie cut into small little pieces, you are buying a share of that pie or a slice of that pie. You would own a portion of McDonald's if you buy shares of McDonald's. A very small share but a share, nonetheless. Most people do not buy the whole company, that will be reserved for people like Warren Buffett and the like. But the concept is this, if there are a million shares outstanding and you buy one of those shares or one stock then you are getting one, one-millionth of the company, or you can imagine 1/1,000,000 of a pie. That is the concept of shares and stock so when you're buying shares of stock of a company, you're buying a percentage of the company, a very small percentage, but a percentage nonetheless. A company could have a billion shares outstanding, if you buy one share your share would be one-billionth of that company. The great thing with this is that if the company can make lots of money and pays lots of dividends, you get a share of those dividends so if the company decides to pay out a billion dollars in dividends and has one billion shares outstanding you would get $1 per share of those dividends for each share you own.

What's the difference between a stock and a share? When people talk about stock and shares for the most part these two are used interchangeably and for this book, we will use them interchangeably, as well. But if you think about it in general terms a company has stocks this is the smallest fraction or share of a company that you can purchase. You are actually buying stocks which give you a share of a company. The number of stocks that are issued by the company will determine what share each stock is worth or what fraction they are purchasing. There are the 2 categories of stock, there are issued stocks and there are outstanding stocks. The issued stock is basically the number of shares authorized and the outstanding stocks are the number of shares that are owned by investors. The issued or authorized shares, by definition, must be greater than the outstanding shares.

Shares is a portion of a company and the smallest share of the company is one stock. You cannot buy half a share or half a stock in a company.

Preferred Stock versus Common Stock
The difference between Common Shares and Preferred Shares are that the common shares have voting rights and preferred shares do not have voting rights. The other major difference is that the preferred shares have a guaranteed amount of dividend income, much like loans, these dividends must be paid to the preferred shareholders before any income can go to the common shareholders. Common shares are a form of equity, however, the preferred share has some traits that are like equity but because the payments are guaranteed just as a payment with a loan, it has some traits that are similar to a liability. These payments are guaranteed as such preferred shares can be halfway between a loan and equity.

Bonds
Bonds are a form of financing for a company. A company can issue bonds and get further funding for the company. When you look at the balance sheet of a company we see three main items we see the assets, the liabilities, and the equity section. Bonds belong to the liability section on the balance sheet and forms part of the total liabilities. It is a financing tool for the company. So instead of issuing more equity as a way to finance the company, the company issues more debt. Let's say the company needs to fund another hundred mil-

lion dollars of assets they can do so in two ways they can issue debt in the form of bonds or they can issue more equity. Another form of a liability would be a bank loan. However, when the company wants to find a lot of funding they can start to issue bonds, the difference between a bond and a bank loan is the bonds are issued to the public and the bank loans are issued by the bank.

The other main difference is the rates, the idea with the bond is that the company can raise sufficient funding to the public, and at a lower than the rate they can find at the bank. If the company could get the same rate or a lower rate with the bank then they would most likely go with the bank. The bank will charge more to the company than the company will issue to the public. A small difference in rates can have a significant effect. If the loan is small, they will go with the bank, as it is faster and the difference it rates will not play a major role. However, if they are looking for a significant amount of funding, then a small difference in rates will make a large difference. The idea is the company can save a small amount by going through the public versus going with a bank. If there is a lot of debt involved even a 1% or a 2% difference in rates can have a significant effect on the bottom line of the company. There may also be cases where the bank does not want to issue so much debt and that will force the company to issue bonds.

Balance sheet
It is important to understand that the balance sheet is formed by the formula assets = liabilities + equity. This is one of the basic formulas in accounting and any shareholder or any person looking to invest in stocks should understand what a balance sheet is. So a company is going to earn profit by employing its assets. You use your assets to derive profits. For example, if you're selling smartphones you going to use your assets to produce them and then to start selling them and you will be selling your inventory which is also an asset, these assets will drive your profits.

Financial statements of a company
There are two main financial statements of a company your balance sheet and your income statement. These are two of the most critical statements and they should be well understood. The balance sheet tells you what your assets, liabilities, and equity are at a given point in time. While the income statement shows your profits and losses. It shows your revenues and your expenses to get to your bottom line, or your net profit or net loss for a given period, usually for the year ending as at a specific date.

Financial Statements
There are other important financial statements such as the statement of changes in financial posi-

tion or the cash flow statement. This is important to see where the cash flow is coming in and whether cash is not coming in. This would be important to see if there's a potential cash flow problem with the company. Cash flow problems with a company can cause serious problems, if they can't get cash on time to pay off their debts then it is possible that even though the company has great potential if it cannot pay its debt as they come due, it may go bankrupt. Any company that does not have enough cash flowing in could result in serious consequences. The company must have enough cash flow to pay its debts otherwise the company will not be able to maintain a going concern. In terms of investing and with most financial statements, you will be assuming that the company is a going concern. Hence, they do not have a cash flow issue. They are able to pay off their debts as they come due. The main reason to use the cash flow statement is to determine that this assumption is true.

The income statement can be used to get an estimate of the company's value. If a company would have no future profits then that company would have no value basically.

Value of a Company

The main way to value a company is to look at the overall profits it will have. You would use the net present value of the future profits into perpetuity and then determine the price, or the value of this company. If a company has zero profits over the next 20, 30, or 50 years then that company will have zero value. If that is the case, that the company has no outlook for future profits then the value of the company immediately refers to its balance sheet value or basically the assets less the liabilities which is equal to the equity. You should pay no more than the value of the equity, but this will mean, you get no profits, hence, you should not invest here.

Book Value

On the balance sheet, another important item is your equity the equity is basically the assets less liabilities. Basically, this is the book value of your shares. So if you have a million outstanding shares and your equity is sitting at 20 million dollars then your equity per share is $20. That's 20 million dollars / 1 million shares is equal to $20. This can also be called the book value.

Earnings Per Share (EPS)

Earnings per share, this is another very important ratio your EPS or your earnings per share is basically the total amount of earnings, which you would find on your income statement, and then divided by the total number shares outstanding. If a company has earned $100 M in 2019 and they have 10 million shares outstanding then that would have an EPS of $100 million / 10 million which is equal to $10 per share. This means that each share has a percentage of the total net income and that percentage would be the EPS so that would be their earnings per share. In this case, the EPS would be $10 per share. So if you are holding a hundred shares then your share of the profits would be 100 times $10, you would earn roughly $1,000. Some of this may be paid to you in the form of dividends and the rest of this would be reinvested into the company, to earn even more profits next year.

Dividends

Dividends are important for the investor because it is a way of having cash flow. If a company does not issue any dividends then there is no cash flow for the investor and the only way to have a cash flow is for the investor to sell some of the shares. This can be a bit of a liability for an investor if the only way that he or she is going to profit is by selling shares. Now, it is not a total no go zone because you could have a company that's so good but they increase their value by 15% per year. Even without paying a dividend, this rate of return is very significant. As such, you need to look at both dividends and growth together rather than separately. You also need to consider your investment goals. With a company that does not pay dividends, the investor can still make a profit, by selling a small portion of those shares. However, if you think about it, it's preferable to have a company that increases in value by 10% to 15% per year and issues no dividends than a company that grows at 5% to 6% per year and issues a 1% to 2% dividends per year. Keep this in mind when comparing dividend-paying stocks to non-dividend paying stocks.

The nice concept of dividends is really that you do not have to sell the shares and you can still get a profit from your investment, a profit in the form of cash so if you're using your stocks as a way to retire this is a way that you could have a cash flow in your retirement years without having to sell off your shares.

Price-earnings ratio or PE ratio

The price-earnings or PE ratio is really the ratio between the price of the shares divided by the earnings of the shares. So if the shares are trading at $100 per share and you have an EPS $10 per share then your PE ratio would be a 100 / 10 or 10. Your PE ratio would be 10. So this means you are paying 10 times the earnings for the price of your shares. The key ratios can vary greatly between stocks. The reasons for these variances can be determined from a number of reasons, the first is that you are expecting great growth, when you are expecting great growth, your earnings today is going to be a far lower than your earnings three, four, or five years down the road.

Hence, you are paying a premium on your earnings and the PE ratios can grow greatly in magnitude to 50 or 60. The other way for a very high PE ratio is where your earnings for this year was extremely small but the value of your company has not decreased. For example, if you're normally earning a $100 M per year but something happened this year or the company was doing some major revisions or there was an event outside of the company's control. But, the company had predicted that they would only earn $10 M. You can still have the same value of the company then you would have a very small EPS the EPS could drop down to $1 per share, but the value of the company would not be that much different.

The company would still have a value of a hundred dollars per share but now you're EPS is $1. Your PE ratio now increases to 100. This is another way to have a very high PE ratio. In other words, you had a great dip in your earnings but there was not a significant or related reduction in the valuation of the company and the dip was just a temporary change in your earnings. That can create a very large PE ratio. If the change in your earnings was significant and that caused a permanent decrease in the value of the company then what would happen is there would be a great decrease in the price of your stock and your PE ratio would change a lot less. In this situation, both the value of the company and the EPS would go down, this would cause less of a change in the PE ratio.

Investing

Now let's get to the actual investing piece. The first step you will need to do within the next few days is to create an actual account and create a dummy account. You should create the actual account so that when you are ready, you can dive right in, but as well, you could delay this for some time.

You should understand what kind of investor you would like to be, hold for the long term or day trading would be your two extremes. We do not recommend day trading for the beginner. This is for a more advanced level trader, but we do have a book on that, so if interested, we break it down into simple steps. For now, your main goal will be to be an investor for the long term. The next couple of books will demonstrate ways to become a trader, but you need to have the basics first and some experience first.

CHAPTER 3 - TIME VALUE OF MONEY

To fully understand investing it is important to understand the time value of money and compound interest. If you can invest funds at a fixed interest rate or fixed rate of return for several years, you can experience exponential growth of your portfolio.

If you can get an average of about 8% return per year, then your doubling period will be about nine to ten years and if you can get a 10% return, your doubling period would be about eight years. We will compare values while looking at 8% return versus 12% return.

If you invest $24,000 per year or $2,000 per month, you can have a significant sum at retirement, if you do this consistently and can get a consistent return.

We will compare the results on a portfolio that is invested over 40 years at $24,000 per year. For simplicity, we will assume that the funds are all contributed right at the end of the year. While the results would be higher if they are invested each month.

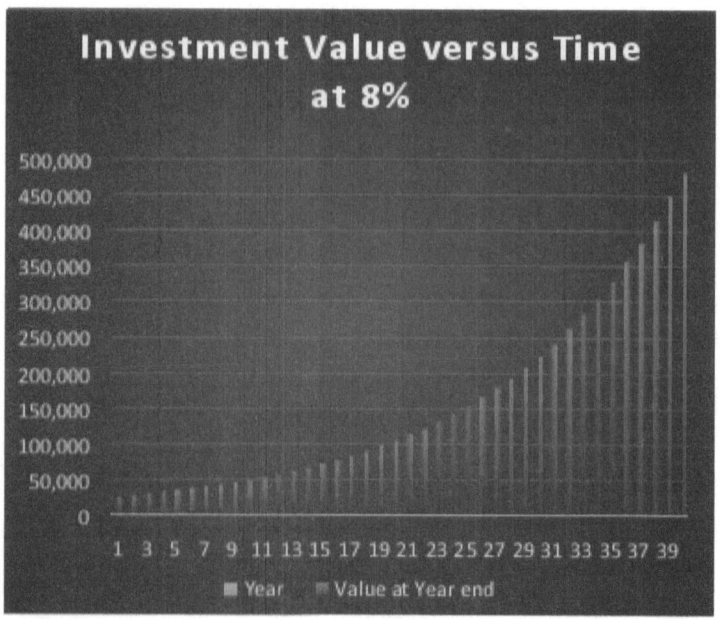

This chart shows us that after 40 years at 8% growth, the amount of $24,000 is worth almost $482,000 this is 20 times the original value. The investment has gained over $458,000, which is almost the same amount of growth as investing an additional $12,000 per year.

Rate of Return at 12%

Let us compare this to the 12% rate of return.

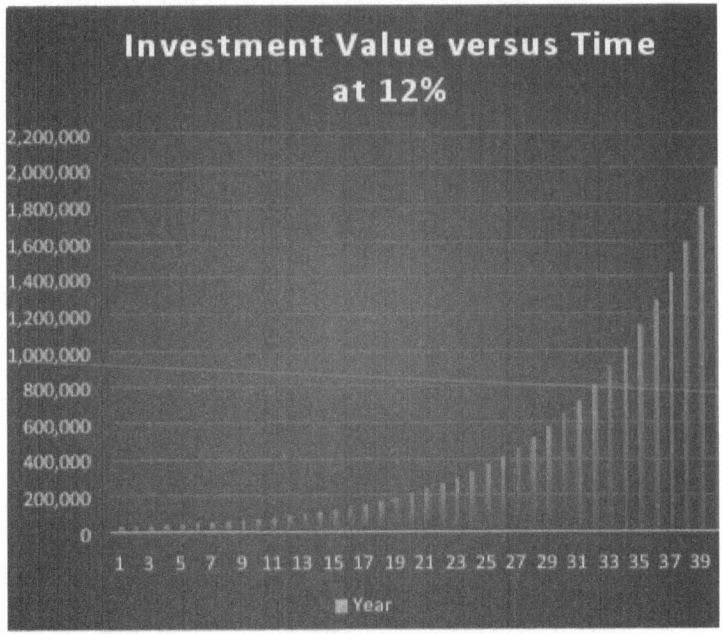

Here you can see that $24,000 is now worth $2,000,000 in 40 years which is significantly more than the value at 8%, one can see that a small increase here can have a significant increase in results.

Rate of Return at 25%

Let us see the same results at 25%, but now we will only be investing $1,000 per year.

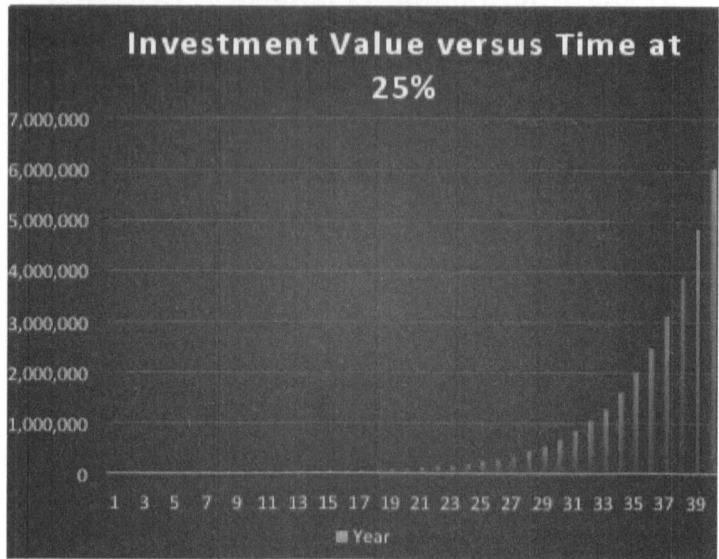

What you see here is a staggering growth. $1,000 has turned into $6,000,000 in forty years. This is a growth of 6,000 times the original amount. If the original investment was $24,000, the final sum would be $124,000,000. This sustained growth at 25% is not very realistic, but it is important to demonstrate how exponential growth can effect your portfolio and how a small change in the growth rate can have a significant effect on the overall portfolio.

Cumulative Investment at 8%

The important thing with the time value of money is that you can see how quickly things can grow. For now, let's focus on the 8% growth chart. You can see here that the growth is quite significant. If we look at the cumulative growth at the contribution of $2,000 per month over 40 years, we can see that the end value is over $6 million. If we look at the chart we'll see that the investment profit is $5,257,000.

We can see at 40 years, you will have a portfolio value of $6.217 million. And that's on a contribution of $960,000. So a significant portion of that is pure profit, over 80% of that portfolio is coming from profit and not from the contributions.

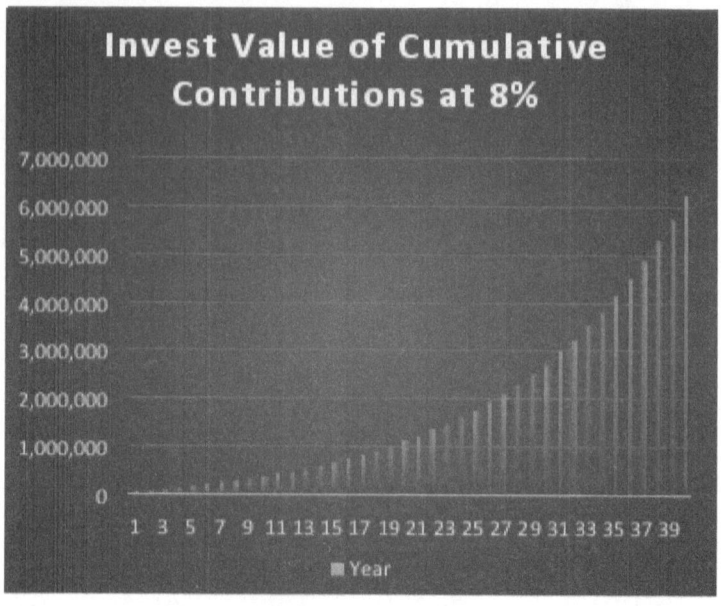

So this is important to consider this means that the vast majority of your portfolio is now coming from profit. And if you have a portfolio of about $6.2 million. Let's say you're earning 8% on that. That's over $480,000 per year. So you can retire quite comfortably. And if you look at the 30-year mark, it's also interesting to see at year 30 you see you have a total portfolio of about $2.7 million. And that's on a total contribution of $720,000. So, the profit of that is about $2.0 million. That's a very good profit. And in fact, if we look at that. If you were to retire at year 30, you would have $2.7 million. So let's say you're earning 8% interest you would have revenues of over $200,000 per year. This is far greater than the average salary and much higher than even good salaries. So you could retire quite comfortably at $200,000 per year or earning 8% per year. And if you're earning, let's say 4% in dividends, you'd be earning over $100,000 per year. That's a very good return plus you'd be increasing your portfolio by $100,000 per year. So you would be definitely in good shape.

Here is the chart showing exact figures per year

Year	Investment	Value at Year end	Cumulative Investment	Total invested	Investment profit
		Investment at 8%			
1	24,000	24,000	24,000	24,000	0
2	24,000	25,920	49,920	48,000	1,920
3	24,000	27,994	77,914	72,000	5,914
4	24,000	30,233	108,147	96,000	12,147
5	24,000	32,652	140,798	120,000	20,798
6	24,000	35,264	176,062	144,000	32,062
7	24,000	38,085	214,147	168,000	46,147
8	24,000	41,132	255,279	192,000	63,279
9	24,000	44,422	299,701	216,000	83,701
10	24,000	47,976	347,677	240,000	107,677
11	24,000	51,814	399,492	264,000	135,492
12	24,000	55,959	455,451	288,000	167,451
13	24,000	60,436	515,887	312,000	203,887
14	24,000	65,271	581,158	336,000	245,158
15	24,000	70,493	651,651	360,000	291,651
16	24,000	76,132	727,783	384,000	343,783
17	24,000	82,223	810,005	408,000	402,005
18	24,000	88,800	898,806	432,000	466,806
19	24,000	95,904	994,710	456,000	538,710
20	24,000	103,577	1,098,287	480,000	618,287
21	24,000	111,863	1,210,150	504,000	706,150
22	24,000	120,812	1,330,962	528,000	802,962
23	24,000	130,477	1,461,439	552,000	909,439
24	24,000	140,915	1,602,354	576,000	1,026,354
25	24,000	152,188	1,754,543	600,000	1,154,543
26	24,000	164,363	1,918,906	624,000	1,294,906
27	24,000	177,512	2,096,418	648,000	1,448,418
28	24,000	191,713	2,288,132	672,000	1,616,132
29	24,000	207,051	2,495,182	696,000	1,799,182
30	24,000	223,615	2,718,797	720,000	1,998,797
31	24,000	241,504	2,960,301	744,000	2,216,301
32	24,000	260,824	3,221,125	768,000	2,453,125
33	24,000	281,690	3,502,815	792,000	2,710,815
34	24,000	304,225	3,807,040	816,000	2,991,040
35	24,000	328,563	4,135,603	840,000	3,295,603
36	24,000	354,848	4,490,452	864,000	3,626,452
37	24,000	383,236	4,873,688	888,000	3,985,688
38	24,000	413,895	5,287,583	912,000	4,375,583
39	24,000	447,007	5,734,589	936,000	4,798,589
40	24,000	482,767	6,217,356	960,000	5,257,356

Cumulative Investment at 12%

Now let's compare that to 12%. This rate of return doesn't sound like a great difference from the 8% return but look at the difference in the numbers. Now we're also going to assume that we're contributing the same amount $24,000 per year, here we'll see that at the end of 40 years, you'll have a portfolio value of $18.4 million and that's on total contributions of $960,000. That means, almost $17.5 million of pure profit.

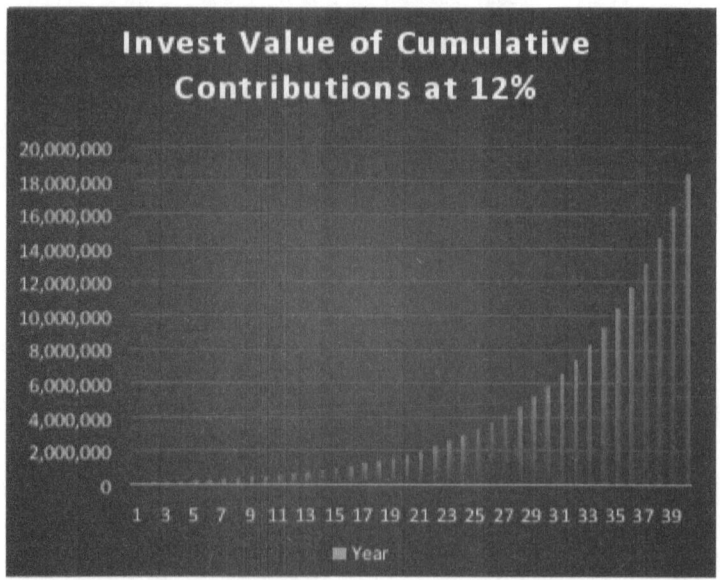

If you were to retire at that point. Let's say you

were to earn 10% per year you would have $1.8 million per year of profits. This is much more than most people would need to retire. Now let's go to year 30, at year 30 we would see that you would have a portfolio size of $5.8 million on a contribution of $720 K, which is over $5 M in profit. If you retire with a portfolio $5.8 million and you're earning 10% per year, that's $580,000 per year that you can retire on. That's a very significant revenue stream. So, you can easily retire after 30 years if you're earning 12% per year on average.

Here is the chart showing exact figures per year:

Year	Investment	Investment at 12%		Total invested	Investment profit
		Value at Year end	Cumulative Investment		
1	24,000	24,000	24,000	24,000	0
2	24,000	26,880	50,880	48,000	2,880
3	24,000	30,106	80,986	72,000	8,986
4	24,000	33,718	114,704	96,000	18,704
5	24,000	37,764	152,468	120,000	32,468
6	24,000	42,296	194,765	144,000	50,765
7	24,000	47,372	242,136	168,000	74,136
8	24,000	53,056	295,193	192,000	103,193
9	24,000	59,423	354,616	216,000	138,616
10	24,000	66,554	421,170	240,000	181,170
11	24,000	74,540	495,710	264,000	231,710
12	24,000	83,485	579,195	288,000	291,195
13	24,000	93,503	672,699	312,000	360,699
14	24,000	104,724	777,422	336,000	441,422
15	24,000	117,291	894,713	360,000	534,713
16	24,000	131,366	1,026,079	384,000	642,079
17	24,000	147,129	1,173,208	408,000	765,208
18	24,000	164,785	1,337,993	432,000	905,993
19	24,000	184,559	1,522,552	456,000	1,066,552
20	24,000	206,706	1,729,259	480,000	1,249,259
21	24,000	231,511	1,960,770	504,000	1,456,770
22	24,000	259,292	2,220,062	528,000	1,692,062
23	24,000	290,407	2,510,469	552,000	1,958,469
24	24,000	325,256	2,835,726	576,000	2,259,726
25	24,000	364,287	3,200,013	600,000	2,600,013
26	24,000	408,002	3,608,014	624,000	2,984,014
27	24,000	456,962	4,064,976	648,000	3,416,976
28	24,000	511,797	4,576,773	672,000	3,904,773
29	24,000	573,213	5,149,986	696,000	4,453,986
30	24,000	641,998	5,791,984	720,000	5,071,984
31	24,000	719,038	6,511,023	744,000	5,767,023
32	24,000	805,323	7,316,345	768,000	6,548,345
33	24,000	901,961	8,218,307	792,000	7,426,307
34	24,000	1,010,197	9,228,503	816,000	8,412,503
35	24,000	1,131,420	10,359,924	840,000	9,519,924
36	24,000	1,267,191	11,627,115	864,000	10,763,115
37	24,000	1,419,254	13,046,369	888,000	12,158,369
38	24,000	1,589,564	14,635,933	912,000	13,723,933
39	24,000	1,780,312	16,416,245	936,000	15,480,245
40	24,000	1,993,949	18,410,194	960,000	17,450,194

Some of these ETFs and some of the stocks for example Berkshire Hathaway has shown for a long period that they can earn well over 12%. So if you had invested 30 years ago in Berkshire Hathaway, and you had invested $24,000 per year, you would now be looking at more than $5.8 million sitting in your portfolio. So this is the way to win in investing, and this is the way to succeed. So, it's about understanding the time value of money, and how there's exponential growth when you hold investments for the long term. This is why they do so well. Now if we look at the very unrealistic, but it's important to compare if we earn 25% per year. Now, here we're only looking at a $1,000 investment per year because the growth rate is so high. After 40 years if you earn 25% per year, you would have an investment portfolio value of $30 million. You would have invested $40,000, that's $1,000 per year. So, all of that 99% of that is pure profit, you'd be looking at $30 million of profit.

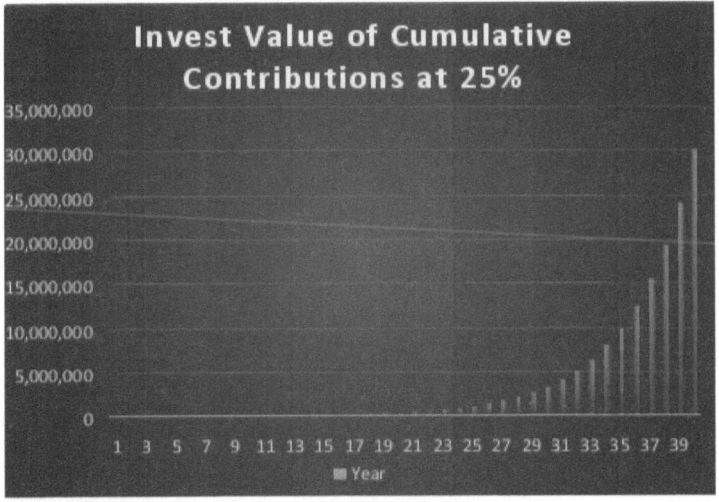

The reason this is so significant is that 25% is a very, very large number and in fact, with 25% the doubling rate gets very short, hence it doubles very quickly. If we look at the doubling rate at 25%, it is just about every four years it would double. So that's a really quick doubling rate at 8% it's about every 10 years so that means the number of times it doubles is quite significant. And you can see the value here is $30 million. After 40 years, with only investing $40,000. So, quite a several times difference. If we go to 30 years we can see that the value is $3 million. You can see quite a difference 10 times in the last 10 years.

Over 10 years, the total investment portfolio multiplied almost by 10.

Here is the Chart for 25% growth:

		Investment at 25%			
Year	Investment	Value at Year end	Cumulative Investment	Total invested	Investment profit
1	1,000	1,000	1,000	1,000	0
2	1,000	1,250	2,250	2,000	250
3	1,000	1,563	3,813	3,000	813
4	1,000	1,953	5,766	4,000	1,766
5	1,000	2,441	8,207	5,000	3,207
6	1,000	3,052	11,259	6,000	5,259
7	1,000	3,815	15,073	7,000	8,073
8	1,000	4,768	19,842	8,000	11,842
9	1,000	5,960	25,802	9,000	16,802
10	1,000	7,451	33,253	10,000	23,253
11	1,000	9,313	42,566	11,000	31,566
12	1,000	11,642	54,208	12,000	42,208
13	1,000	14,552	68,760	13,000	55,760
14	1,000	18,190	86,949	14,000	72,949
15	1,000	22,737	109,687	15,000	94,687
16	1,000	28,422	138,109	16,000	122,109
17	1,000	35,527	173,636	17,000	156,636
18	1,000	44,409	218,045	18,000	200,045
19	1,000	55,511	273,556	19,000	254,556
20	1,000	69,389	342,945	20,000	322,945
21	1,000	86,736	429,681	21,000	408,681
22	1,000	108,420	538,101	22,000	516,101
23	1,000	135,525	673,626	23,000	650,626
24	1,000	169,407	843,033	24,000	819,033
25	1,000	211,758	1,054,791	25,000	1,029,791
26	1,000	264,698	1,319,489	26,000	1,293,489
27	1,000	330,872	1,650,361	27,000	1,623,361
28	1,000	413,590	2,063,952	28,000	2,035,952
29	1,000	516,988	2,580,939	29,000	2,551,939
30	1,000	646,235	3,227,174	30,000	3,197,174
31	1,000	807,794	4,034,968	31,000	4,003,968
32	1,000	1,009,742	5,044,710	32,000	5,012,710
33	1,000	1,262,177	6,306,887	33,000	6,273,887
34	1,000	1,577,722	7,884,609	34,000	7,850,609
35	1,000	1,972,152	9,856,761	35,000	9,821,761
36	1,000	2,465,190	12,321,952	36,000	12,285,952
37	1,000	3,081,488	15,403,440	37,000	15,366,440
38	1,000	3,851,860	19,255,299	38,000	19,217,299
39	1,000	4,814,825	24,070,124	39,000	24,031,124
40	1,000	6,018,531	30,088,655	40,000	30,048,655

That's a significant increase. And if you're looking to retire at year 30, you could easily retire after 30 years especially if you're earning 25%. Let's say you're only earning 10%. Well, you'd be retiring with $300,000 per year. So this is a very good result. And this is the why time value of money is so important. You need to understand these concepts because the way you succeed in investing is holding it for the long term. So the main reason to succeed is by putting new investments in. If you're investing each year. And you're investing for the long term.

So that means you're never selling.

You might be transitioning from one stock to another you might sell the one you might buy another, but the end goal is you're doing very little sales and mostly what you're doing is you're adding into your portfolio, you need to consistently add to your portfolio, and you need to consistently let it sit there to grow. That's the way the ETF strategy works. And that's the way you can follow these charts and increase your profits and portfolio. Now it's very important to note that you're going to have some years where you lose, maybe 5%, maybe 10% - that's okay because in some years you will gain 25% and in some years you will gain 12%. Some years you will lose 10%. That's normal. What you need to do is not get your emotions caught up when you're looking at losses. With investing, gains and losses are part of the normal course of business. What you cannot do is panic and pull your money out and incur many more losses. You need to play cool and you need to not let your emotions run wild. If you let your emotions get the better of you you will make mistakes and you will lose profits and incur losses.

CHAPTER 4 - SETTING GOALS

"AN INVESTOR WITHOUT INVESTMENT OBJECT-
IVES IS LIKE A TRAVELER WITHOUT A DESTIN-
ATION."

- ANONYMOUS

Setting goals is a very important process in investing. Your goals must be realistic and they must be achievable. For example, if your goal is to start with $100 and have a million dollars next month, well this is not going to be achievable and is not going to be reasonable. You are better off buying lottery tickets to achieve that purpose. But we do not recommend that because that is a very likely loss.

What is Achievable?
What is achievable is anything from a rate of 6% to 15%, per year. The lower the rate, then the more achievable it is and the less risky, the higher

rate is also achievable, but with a little bit higher risk. So we recommend aiming towards 8% to 12%, which is a good high return and still maintaining relatively low risk. You can look at our charts and you can see how much you can earn for 20, 30 or 40 years. Each year if you were to invest a fixed amount per year.

So if you were to invest. $2,000 every month and you were to do this for 30 years. Then at the end of 30 years, you could have a portfolio worth between $2.5 M and $5.7 M, depending on the rate of return.

So when you look at that, that's investing $24,000, per year. And if you're doing this over 30 years that is $720,000, in terms of investment money.

Earning Significant Investment Revenue

But that money will earn a significant amount of investment revenue during this time and coupled with the investment sum, you will now have $3 to $5 million in your portfolio when you have invested only $750,000 so this is a great return. This is how you can achieve financial freedom and how you can gain with investing, and how you can be a successful investor.

Reasonable Goals

The first thing you need to do is keep your goals reasonable and keep your goals achievable, then find out how you are going to achieve those goals. So if you want to have a portfolio of $5 million in 10 years, then you're going to need to invest a certain amount every year to achieve that. So this is the thing that you need to start thinking about, to make your goals achievable. It is impossible for this book, to be able to put every goal and every rate of return. That is possible. So what we've done is the next best thing, we have a link at the back of this book and on our site where you can estimate your return given certain parameters. And you can find out if your goals are achievable and what rate of return would you need to achieve that goal. Over the next number of years, you must adhere to your plan, in terms of investing and strategy.

Have a Plan
It is good to have a strategy and a plan, but you must also follow them. So please use this website to then determine if your goals are achievable or not. You can use this website free of charge. We do not charge you anything and it is our gift to you, and we would love to hear from you if your what your goals are and how we can help you to achieve them.

Write out your Goals
If you put a goal of I am going to invest X amount per year for the next 10 years or the next 20 years, whatever it is, then we will tell you what rate of return, you will need, and if that rate of

return falls between 8% to 12%, then that means your goal is achievable. We will find ways to work with you to be able to get that for you. Now, you will not achieve your goal, if you do not follow your plan. So for example, if you plan on investing $36,000 per year or $3,000 per month.

Follow your Plan

But then you end up only investing $500 this month $1,000 the next month and who knows what else, then one month perhaps you put in $3,000. Well, you are not going to achieve your goal. You need to follow your plan, otherwise, you won't achieve the results you desire. This is called paying yourself first. So for example, if you plan on investing $3,000 per month for the next 30 years, then what you need to do is the first $3,000 that you've received from your employment income or your business income, that amount goes directly to your investment account, and you start investing, as you have planned. This means that you must have a steady income and you must be able to pay yourself first, and also pay off all of your monthly costs. So if you're earning $5,000 per month, and your monthly expenses are $3,000 per month. You are not going to be able to invest $3,000 per month, you will be short $1,000 per month. So make sure that your plan is reasonable. Consider what your monthly costs are and your monthly revenues. On the other hand, you could be able to invest $2,000 per month, but then you would need to see how much time you would need to have for you to have a retirement day.

This is the main goal of creating a plan. So, set out your goals. Let us say that you would like to retire by the time you're 55 you're now 35, you've got 20 years to retire. How much can you put in every month? Okay, so you can put in anywhere from $2,000 to $4,000. Well, what do you have to sacrifice to make it $4,000, what will be the result of you putting in only $2,000 per month? How much will you have at the end when you turn 55? When you turn 55 if you go with $4,000 per month, how much will you have in your portfolio? What if you retire at 60 instead? These are all things that you need to consider while setting up your investment goals.

CHAPTER 5 - INVESTMENTS

"IF INVESTING IS ENTERTAINING, IF YOU'RE HAV-
ING FUN, YOU'RE PROBABLY NOT MAKING ANY
MONEY. GOOD INVESTING IS BORING."

- GEORGE SOROS

Investments are a critical tool to ensure one's financial future. This is an area that if you follow the lessons in this book, this will likely be the largest source of your income over your lifetime. In the first part of your career, your earnings will be mostly derived from employment income, then it will move to business income or perhaps rental income but over time, this should be your number one source of income.

In this chapter we will show you how to invest those savings, then not too far into the future, there will be a time where your investment income earns more per year than your salary, this will continue and if you start early enough, your investment income may be about ten times your employment income.

Type of Investments
What type of instruments do we advocate to use and which methodology? We do not advocate day trading, we advocate the polar opposite to day trading. The best and most successful strategy is to buy and hold for the long term. Only sell when you must. This is a critical concept. Whatever investments you purchase are to be held for many years or the rest of your life or at least until retirement age. When you decide to retire, you must have enough income coming in to meet your monthly needs. This can be done by holding investments that pay dividends or it can be achieved by selling off some of your investments. Remember that both dividend income and selling will have some tax implications which will require you to incorporate this into your calculations.

Long Term Trading versus Short Term
We must advocate strongly towards investing for the long term and against day trading, especially for the beginner. If you are very inclined towards day-trading, we will have a book on that very soon, but do understand that there are far more risks involved and we do not recommend this

strategy for the beginner. Any day trading can be done with your funds that you can throw away. Look at it as if it were a highly risky venture. We are not saying not to do this, but do not have this negatively affect your true investment, which will safely guarantee your future. If you are becoming a successful day trader, then you can look to supplementing your investment with any earnings from this activity. This area is highly speculative and as such it is also highly risky, only use funds that you are willing to lose. As well, start day trading with a dummy account, not using real funds.

Diversify

You have most likely heard the expression, "Do not put all your eggs in one basket." We also advocate this when it comes to investing. It is for that reason that for beginners we advocate to invest in index funds, such as Dow Jones, S&P 500 or NAS-DAQ (National Association of Securities Dealers Automated Quotations). What we advocate for are both Exchange Traded Fund (ETF) and Index funds for now in one of the three markets.

One area to think about when investing are the fees, this is critical. What are the fees associated with a purchase, is that fee acceptable. If you have a $5 fee on a $1,000 investment, this would be fine, anything less than 1% is decent but aim towards getting this at zero or close to zero, 0.1%

is very acceptable. If you are gearing towards an index fund, this is similar to a mutual fund, but it has much fewer fees than an actively traded fund.

Actively Traded Fund versus Passively Traded Fund

Both of these are mutual funds, there is a significant distinction between the two, the actively traded funds have fund managers that actively make trades with the hope of beating the market. The problem is that these trades incur costs and those costs are passed on to the consumer. As well, it is very rare for a fund manager to beat the market, hence, despite being well paid and incurring more fees they still are outperformed by the market. Conversely, a passively traded fund follows set rules and does not make many trades during the year. This fund is set to match the market, hence, its fees are lower and those savings are passed to the consumer. As well, they meet the market, hence, they generally outperform the actively traded funds. Does that mean that you should avoid actively traded mutual funds? For beginners in investing our recommendation would be to avoid those funds and stick to lower-cost funds, with less risk and more likelihood to meet market gains as opposed to those that are likely to be outperformed by the market.

Index Fund vs ETF

How should one decide between an index fund

and an ETF? An index fund is a mutual fund with a very low costs ratio, in other words, you will not be charged much for annual costs, this could be as low as 0.1%, which is an acceptable level, an actively traded one can have costs as high as 1% or ten times as much, these should be avoided for now.

Exchange Traded Fund (ETF)

The ETF has even less fees and is similar to buying a stock of each of the stocks within the market. Their fees can be as low as 0.05% per year, which is extremely reasonable and acceptable. One also needs to include the cost of purchasing an ETF versus the cost of purchasing an index fund. The index fund may have lower costs in this regard and one would need to combine the two to see which is better. In the long run, having a lower annual cost will pay huge dividends (no pun intended) down the road. If we are assuming an 8% return for the index fund, then the ETF may have a return of 8.5%, this will have a great difference down the road. The future value of $1,000 at 8% in 20 years will have a value of $4,661, while the same investment for the same time at 8.5% will have a value of $5,112, which is almost 10% more. Hence, we are strongly advocating to use ETF with the lowest expense ratio.

For more advanced investors we will go into much further detail in another book and speak more about the differences on our website. Our recommendations are geared towards both the beginner investor and the typical investor. There are reasons to use actively traded funds, but you have to understand fully the pros and cons. As well, many day-traders are making a healthy living, however, you must be very well versed in trading to do so. Our recommendations are not for those readers.

For this book, we will focus on some well known Exchange Traded Funds (ETF), while we also recommend Index Funds, our focus is on ETF's due to their lower expense ratios over time.

We will look at the following: S&P 500, Dow Jones and NASDAQ, as well, we will add in Berkshire Hathaway (BRK-A), while not an ETF, it does carry a portfolio of stocks and hence it is also less risky since it follows the rule of not putting all of your eggs in one basket.

We have gathered data for each of these over time, some going back over 50 years, we have graphed it out for you. Since we are going so far back, we are graphing the data on January 1 each year. You can also do this every month or even every day. You will get a similar graph but more movement during the year, of course.

Standard and Poor 500 (S&P 500)

You can see a sharp rise in later years. This is typical of an exponential growth curve, it slopes quickly upward. In the early years, there is slow relative growth and then later it grows more quickly.

Imagine if a stock price doubled every ten years. Let us say the price was $10, in year 0, then ten years later it would be $20, twenty years later it would be at $40, thirty years later it would be at $80 and 50 years later it would be at $160. In the last ten years, it grew by $80, while in the first ten years it only grew by $10. This is the power of investing for a long period and a sure way to build wealth.

Let us look at another market.

Dow Jones

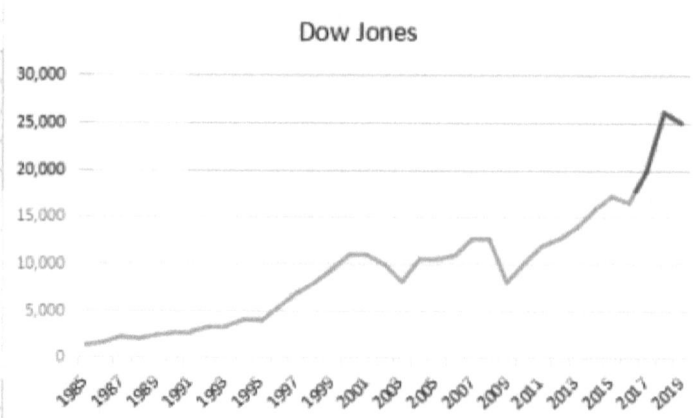

Dow Jones

Similar to the S&P 500, Dow Jones also has an exponential growth curve. This is also a good ETF to hold.

Below is NASDAQ, some consider this one a bit riskier, but over the long term, it shows good strength and strong growth.

NASDAQ

NASDAQ

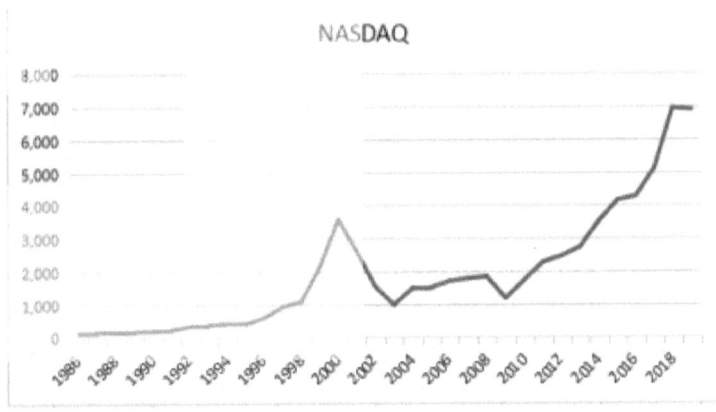

Again, we see strong exponential growth for NAS-DAQ.

It is important to notice that in all of these markets you can see a great drop in around 1999-2000 and around 2008-2009. Without fail each of them displays this drop.

It is important to understand this, there is a risk with each of these markets and stocks in general, however, if you hold these ETF's for 20, 30 years or more, you will be very likely to reduce most of your risk and take advantage of strong growth.

You should also invest regularly and overtime. If a market does fall, then keep buying that market for the next years and you will do well over the long run.

If you made a big investment in 1999 and did not

invest much further, you still will have earned income but you would have earned more by investing in equal portions in 1999, 2000, 2001 and 2002. The same goes for 2008, you would earn a lot more if you invest as markets rise but also invest as markets fall. You may even earn more by investing more as the markets decrease. When a market falls, do not look at this as a loss, look at this as an opportunity. Now, the stock prices are lower and there are more deals available.

It is important to remember that this strategy is to hold for the long term. This way when the value of an ETF falls, do not consider it as a loss but consider that you are now getting a great deal as you invest more. Use this strategy for ETF's do not use it for individual stocks. There is a chance that an individual stock goes to zero or goes bankrupt. The likelihood of a whole market being wiped out is far less likely. There was a great market crash in 1929, but those who invested in the 1930s made fortunes.

Not a Day Trader

You are not a day trader with this strategy so do not sell on the losses. Many people panic and sell as a market loses value, this is exactly what you do not want to do. You want to do the opposite, when others are panicking and selling, this is the time to start buying. When others are buying and rising prices of markets, this is the only time one could consider selling. However, do avoid this urge. You are not day trading, you are holding for the long term.

Let us have a look at Warren Buffett's Berkshire Hathaway stock (BRK-A).

BRK-A

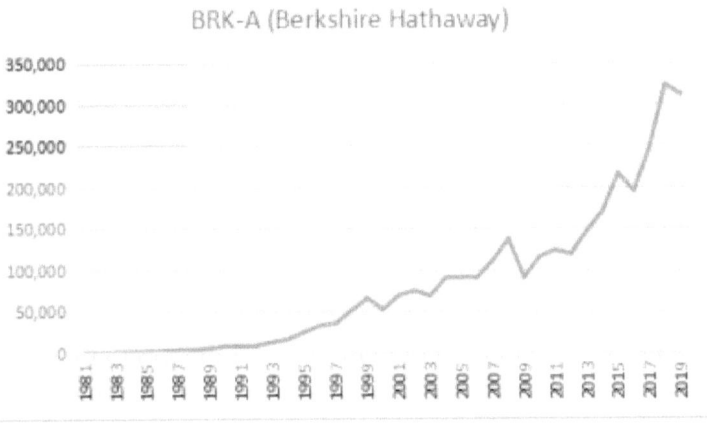

Again, we see a strong exponential growth here. Also, we can see that there were some corrections in 1999 and 2008, but there were far less grave corrections. This is and would be a great stock to own. It is the only non-ETF that we recommend holding. The one concern that we do have is that Warren Buffett is now on the older side, while still healthy, he will not live forever. The stock may have a correction when he does pass away. (We do wish him many more years and much health).

The chart below combines all four of these from 1986 until 2019, to compare these stocks we have set the 1986 value at 100 and put all subsequent values as a ratio of the 1986 price. Hence, their prices are relative to their 1986 value in terms of percent.

Comparison Chart

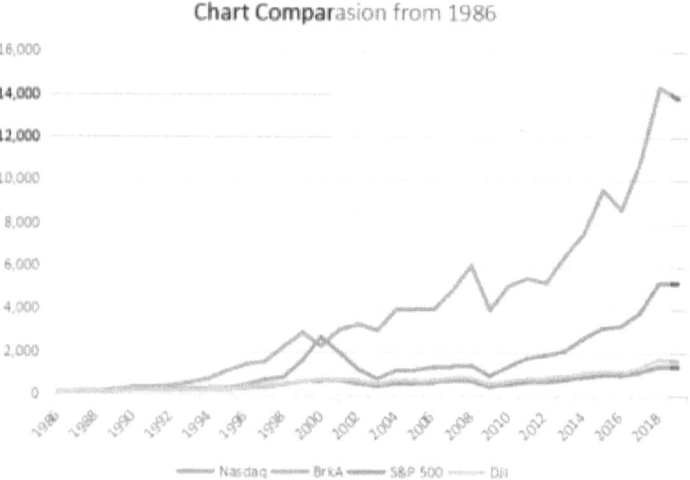

This chart shows all starting at the same value 100, this way we can see the relative growth to each other. BRK-A is the strong winner in this analysis, while NASDAQ also performed quite well, both S&P 500 and Dow Jones were quite similar to Dow Jones having a slight edge on S&P 500.

You can see that there is a great risk with NASDAQ in 2000 - 2003 it lost a lot of value, but over time it recovered and even grew stronger. The growth from 2003 to 2019 was very strong. What is very evident here is the strong growth of BRK-A.

If we look at the 2019 relative values of each, we can see that BRK-A has a relative value of 13,814, this means that it grew a staggering 138 times its starting point since 1986 or in the past 33 years.

If you want to calculate the average annual growth, you can use the Log (base 10 or any base) to calculate that,
To do so, first, calculate the growth, it grew from 100 to 13,814, hence it grew 138.14 times (13,814/100) or (end value/start value). Let us take the Log of that which is 2.1403, now divide that number by the number of years, which is 33. This results in 0.64857. The last step is to put that figure back to 10 to the power of, hence, 10^0.64857 yields a value of 1.1610. If we put that in percentage terms after subtracting one (to get growth) we get a value of 16.1% growth over the past 33 years.

To see if our value is correct, use the following formula:

Start value * (1+ growth rate) ^ number of years therefore 100 * 1.161^33 =13,814.

The formula to calculate the average growth is the

following:

Growth rate ={10 ^[Log (End value/start Value)]/ (number of years)} -1

Following the same formulas, you can see that NASDAQ had a growth rate of 12.7%, while Dow Jones had a rate of 8.7% growth and S&P had a growth rate of 8.0% growth. For this book, we will aim on the side of caution and use a base rate of 8%, but this can be higher.

It is important to practice with these formulas and understand how they work. It is also import-ant to see how a little increase in the average growth rate can have a staggering effect in the long run. The average rate in NASDAQ over the past 33 years is 12.7%, while that of the S&P 500 is 8%, both are strong and respectable growth rates, but if you invested $10,000 in each at the start of 1986, by 2019, your value in NASDAQ would now be $519,000 while your value in S&P 500 would only be $121,000. If this $10,000 was invested in BRK-A, with a growth rate of 16.1%, your value would now be $1,381,000.

Focus on a few Good Exchange-Traded Funds
A good way to start investing would be to focus on these four investment possibilities and focus on holding for the long term. Do not sell, unless there is an urgent need for the funds. Anything that you

buy here should be held until retirement. As well, there are tax implications for selling. Most countries will allow you to avoid paying taxes on any gains until you sell the asset. Then you would have to pay a capital gains tax. We do advocate that you are fair and smart with your taxes. Yes, taxes will need to be paid, but best to leave it to when selling your asset, and the longer you hold on to the stocks, the more taxes you can avoid and pay later down the road.

Each country has a different way to calculate taxes, we advise that you consult with a good CPA to see what are your legal options are to reduce your tax burden.

In summary, we advise going with ETF rather than with individual stocks or mutual funds. The fees attached to mutual funds are very high and those associated with ETF's are quite low. We advise against day-trading and actually advocate for the opposite approach which is holding for the long term and only selling when required or as part of your revenues during retirement.

Active versus Passive
When we look at active trading versus passive trading, we advocate fully on passive trading. Most of the hedge funds or fund experts are on the side of active trading. This makes sense, they are putting years of education and experience to

practice to beat the market. The reality is that most of these do not beat the market. They may beat the market for one year or even two, but over a long period, they lose to the market. Think about the implication of this. In other words, there are hedge fund managers who are paid excessive sums per year who you can beat by simply choosing to invest in a strong ETF as one of the four options that are mentioned here (BRK-A is not an ETF, but a great option to include). This little-understood fact is one that you should always keep in mind. There will be many people advising you to invest in this or that mutual fund. Do resist the urge, put your money in areas where the fees are far less, and where the results are far better. The fees are one of the main reasons that those funds perform worse than the market. Imagine the market performs at 8% with little to no fees, now a hedge fund with a fee of 1%, has to earn 9% just to stay on par. The higher the fees the worse they perform. As well, with active funds there is more chance of sales and buys, also increasing costs and generally under-performing. Stay away from all actively managed funds. If a person could outperform the market, even by 1% or 2%, that person could earn whatever sum they desired.

The only well-known person to be able to achieve these results is Warren Buffett, his net worth is a staggering sum, he is one of the wealthiest people in the world. He follows an approach that is similar and holds for the long term and does not follow day trading. Better to invest in BRK-A or BRK-B than any mutual fund.

CHAPTER 6 -
ETF STRATEGY

With an ETF strategy, the important point is to start investing right away. And what you want to do is set your timeline and set your goals, at the beginning. The great thing with this strategy is it does not involve that much risk as it is highly diversified. In addition to this, it is also a very low-cost endeavor. The ETFs are generally passive investments, which means that their expense ratios are very low. That means you're not paying a high percentage of your profits out to costs, such as investment transactions and also investor management.

With a mutual fund, you're going to be paying a mutual fund manager and this will come at a high price because he or she will be determining which stocks to buy and sell, this person comes at a cost they have an annual salary which can be quite expensive. As well, all those transactions, add up with the transaction costs. These costs are paid by you as fees.

Mutual Fund and ETF
So with a mutual fund, the expense ratio can be quite high, and this can take a toll on your profits. So keep this in mind, the great thing with ETFs, is that they give a very similar return and probably even a better return, and at the same time, they have a very low expense ratio. You could be looking at a difference between 0.1% expense ratio on an ETF, and a 1.5% ratio on a mutual fund. So this can be quite significant, as well, this 1.5% ratio will take a large hit on your profits. Let's say that both the mutual fund and the ETF earned 8%, on returns. Then with the ETF, they're going to charge 0.1% so you'll be left with a 7.9% return on your investment. While if the of the mutual fund had the same return at 8%, then they will take 1.5% of that as costs to manage and you will be left with a return of 6.5%.

This is quite a significant difference compared to the ETF. And if you compound this difference over time the amounts can be extremely significant in 40 years. So keep this in mind when you're looking at the different rates, a very small rate for the expense ratio is the way to go.

Returns on Mutual Funds versus ETF

It is quite well known that most mutual funds, get the same rate of return as an ETF, they generally do not beat the market, which means that if you're in an ETF, which is linked to the market. Then you're going to get a better rate of return than going with mutual funds. So in the first part, you get a better rate of return on the second part you do not get the same amount of fees. So your expense ratio is much lower on the ETF and you are getting a better return. So let's take another example let's say the ETF follows the market and gets a 9% return. But then the mutual fund only gets an 8% return. Plus, they also charge you 1.5% as expenses. So now they are getting 6.5% as a net result for their investors. When you compare this to 9% less their, 0.1% fees, or 8.9%, there's a significant difference from 6.5% to 8.9%.

Effect of small Differences

This could be the difference from ending with a portfolio of $10 million versus ending with a portfolio of $5 million. Assuming the same amount of contributions and the same amount of time being invested.

If you're investing for 40 years and at a consistent rate. Then you could be looking at the difference in 50% of your portfolio, meaning that you could have twice as much in your portfolio. If you went with the 8.9% return versus the 6.5% return. It does not sound like much, at the beginning. But when you add up these small differences and you compound these differences over 40 years. This small difference starts to become significant.

To put this in perspective, if you earn 8.9% per year and invest $24,000 per year, after 40 years, your portfolio will be approximately $7.9 M, while, if you earned 6.5%, your portfolio value would be $4.2 M. This difference is staggering.

ETF Strategy
The ETF strategy is the one that we recommend for every beginner. There are three markets that we recommend, NASDAQ, S&P 500 and Dow Jones. In addition, we recommend investing in Berkshire Hathaway, either BRK-A or BRK-B. Although BRK-B is more accessible to most.

CHAPTER 7
- DIVIDEND
STRATEGY

The dividend strategy is a very important strategy and one that is often used by Warren Buffett. The concept here is that you want to invest in shares that pay dividends. The reason for this is that it is a good idea to invest something where you get a return back. The revenues returned should be in the form of a dividend. If a company does not pay dividends then you will need to sell some of those shares to get a return on the investment, all companies that pay dividends do not require you to sell their shares, in order for you to get some cash flow from these investments.

Cash Flow

The reason this is critical for the investor is that if you want to invest some shares but you also want to use that investment to pay for your retirement costs you need to have a strategy where you are going to receive dividends to cover the cost of your living expenses. You do not want to be put in a situation where you have to sell a part of your portfolio to have funds for your living expenses. If this is the case then there might be a time when you don't want to sell but you are forced to sell. This is the reason that a dividend strategy or dividend-paying stocks have a big advantage. You do not have to sell them, to have a cash flow, while stocks that do not pay dividends, you are forced to sell to have a cash flow.

Suggests Strong Results

Dividend-paying stocks also set an idea that there are strong, or so strong that they can afford to pay dividends without a problem with their cash position. The only drawback with the strategy is that sometimes the company can earn far more with those funds than you might earn if you hold the funds for yourself. Reinvesting these dividends is a good strategy, as well. It really depends on your needs, when you are actively growing your portfolio, you do not need the dividends and they should be reinvested, when you have retired and no longer growing making monthly contributions to your portfolio, this is the time where you would need dividends.

The interesting thing with Warren Buffett and Berkshire Hathaway is that Warren Buffett likes to get shares that pay dividends but he does not want to pay dividends under Berkshire Hathaway. I am a big fan of Warren Buffett and I believe what he espouses and his way of doing things but this has to be one of his little areas that is a bit tricky. I find him to be completely honorable and with a good heart. I would guess that the reason he does not want to pay dividends, is that he believes that he can make far more with this money staying within the company and he is most likely correct. What that means, is if the company does not pay a dividend but those funds were reinvested, then you would earn more, ultimately, than if you had received a dividend. This is something to keep in mind and why paying dividends harms the growth of the company. Many people would like to just reinvest those dividends into the company. However, if you choose several stocks that have dividend-paying you are likely going to be earning a good return and not only that you are earning good cash flow. This cash flow, in many years, will be able to support your financial needs. Hence, if you have a $5 million portfolio and you're earning 3% of dividend income that means you are receiving $150,000 per year to cover your annual costs, as well, your portfolio continues to grow.

Cash Flow and Retirement

The added benefit of creating a cash flow for the dividend-paying stock is definitely worthwhile to consider for those that will be using their investments for retirement. This is likely to encompass the vast majority of investors.

The other idea of investing in dividend-paying stocks is that they will generally outperform others that do not pay dividends. This is true sometimes but not always.

CHAPTER 8 - VALUE INVESTING

"THE INDIVIDUAL INVESTOR SHOULD ACT
CONSISTENTLY AS AN INVESTOR AND NOT AS A
SPECULATOR." - BEN GRAHAM

V alue investing is a very important topic in any investment strategy. It is a great strategy for long term investment and it is one of the two main strategies that we recommend. It is not a perfect strategy for the beginner but it is a strategy that the beginner should be aware of. It would be the ideal second strategy for the beginner. So the first strategy is the ETF strategy which we have outlined in a previous chapter. Then the next strategy is the value investing approach. What we recommend is that you start with the ETF approach and while you are getting comfortable with the ETF approach with real money. You're getting better at this strategy every month, but the reality is, you're following a strategy that is a no-lose strategy, since basically what you're doing is you're following the market, while you're learning this value investing approach. The goal is to build confidence with you as an investor as you are gaining with the ETF approach. You are gaining confidence because you can see that it works.

Learning the Strategy of Value Investing
The next big step is to learn how to do value investing.

You are going to learn this strategy with fake money in a dummy account. The first thing you need to do is to create a dummy account. This will allow you to invest in stocks which you feel have value, but you do not have to risk your real money. If you make losses you will lose in your dummy account, not with your real funds. So what you're going to do is you're going to look at 10 stocks that you like and 10 stocks in markets that you appreciate. You're going to try to value all ten of them.

To learn how to do this you will need to look at our next book in this series, which will have a chapter or two, explaining the techniques that you will need to value, but do get ready for learning this process. It will take you a year or two to get it right, but that's fine in that time your investments in your ETF strategy will be already growing. Remember this is not to replace the ETF strategy. It is rather, in addition to, but not a replacement of the ETF strategy, as well many successful investors will never need to use the value approach of value investing.

Focus on ETF then Value Investing
The reason for this is you can get a very good return with the ETF strategy. But it's very important to understand what value investing is and how it works. So basically the gist of this strategy is you look for strong companies, and you get a valuation of those companies, so you're looking to find the intrinsic value or the true value of the company. This is not an easy thing to do and while a lot of it is science, there's a lot of it that's also a bit of an art. So the idea here is, let's say you knew company XYZ was worth $100 million, and let's say that it was trading at $85, and it had 1 million shares outstanding. Then if you did the market cap you would see that $85 times 1 million shares would be a market cap of $85 million. But you're valuing the company at $100 million so it is selling at a discount. So this would be a company that you would consider buying, you would say that, in your view, the company is worth, $100 per share, for a total market cap of $100 million.

But since it's currently selling trading at $85, that is 15% below your hundred dollar mark, and it would be a time to consider buying. You might decide that you're not going to buy anything that is not selling at a minimum discount of 20%.

In other words, if it's not discounted at least 20% then you're not going to consider buying it. In that case, you would only buy this company if the share price drops below $80.

Setting the Buy Price
But since it's currently at $85 is not that far off and you might even want to put a limit order in so that you buy 100 shares at $80. Then if the stock price drops to $80 you would pick it up. So this is the concept of value investing. You find out the intrinsic price of the company and then you only buy when the price falls below that amount, and you want to set a percent difference. You don't want to buy it at 1% lower than the intrinsic price, you want to buy it at least 20% or 25% below the intrinsic price. So if you calculate the price to be $100, then you would start buying it at either $80 or $75. But you would not buy it above that value. So if the stock is selling or trading at $96, you will not buy. You will wait until it is trading, either at $75 or at $80 depending on if you put 25% or 20% as your limit.

So that's the concept of purchasing with an intrinsic value or with value investing.

Setting the Sell Price

You also have to think about when to sell. It's the same concept but instead of a 25% discount, you might have a 25% surplus. So what that means is you would not sell unless the price is 25% more than the intrinsic price that you calculate. So if you calculate an intrinsic price of $100, then you would not sell it, unless the price were to be above $125.

That is the value investing strategy when it comes to buying and selling. If you think about it, if you look at company XYZ. If you bought at $75, and then you sold it at $125, you would have a $50 gain. And if you did this for 100 shares you would have a profit of $5,000. It may take you one or two years to get there. But the great thing is that this $5,000 gain comes from an investment of $7,500, which is a great return on your investment. That is quite a significant increase in percentage terms. It's $50 divided by $75, which is closing in on a 100% gain. It's a 66.67% gain.

So these are the type of things that you're looking for, you are looking for intrinsic values of good companies that are trading at a discount. You could decide that 25% is too high a discount and you want to make it more like 15% or 10%. Any amount that you feel comfortable with, that's the way you decide when to sell or buy.

Keep a Wide Margin

But 10% would be really at the bare minimum. For example, if you were to go to the extreme and say 1%, then you would be getting into the day trading type margins, and you do not want to be there, not yet. Day trading is for another chapter and another day. We will mention day trading but it is not for the beginner investor. A future book in this series will cover day trading.

CHAPTER 9 - DAY TRADING STRATEGIES

"OCTOBER: THIS IS ONE OF THE PECULIARLY DAN-
GEROUS MONTHS TO SPECULATE IN STOCKS.
THE OTHERS ARE JULY, JANUARY, SEPTEMBER,
APRIL, NOVEMBER, MAY, MARCH, JUNE, DECEM-
BER, AUGUST AND FEBRUARY."

-MARK TWAIN

For the day trader, they must be very cautious. The beginner should not attempt day trading strategies before they have become comfortable with both ETF strategies and value investing strategies. When they are comfortable with purchasing stocks on their own. So for the beginner, it will be several years before they can become a day trader. However, they can practice with this strategy sooner than that, by using a dummy account.

Practice First

Of course, they can try to do a very quick process, but we do not recommend that. First, you got to get a full understanding of what's going on with long term investing. It is important to note that there is a high degree of risk with day trading, in fact much more risk than with long term trading. Or even with individual stock trading, so this is not to be taken on by the beginner. There's a lot of areas where you could lose a lot of money. And you have to understand how you can protect your investments before you start. So every time you do something, you need to find out how you can limit your loss, and how doing that doesn't cause you to have increased losses.

ETF First

Before the beginner starts day trading, they must become an expert with the ETF strategy and they must have demonstrated at least one year of success with the ETF strategy.

If they're interested in pursuing the day trading strategies, then the beginner needs to start with a dummy account. So the first step is to start with a dummy account and practice with that. This way if you have losses and big losses, you won't affect your real money. This will be pretend money, hence it doesn't matter if you win or lose. Once you can demonstrate several successes and perhaps six months in a row of success, then you can start to try it on your own with real funds. But don't try it with a month's investment. Try it with $500 or $1,000, an amount that you're fine with losing. Look at this as an investment for you to learn how to invest in day trading.

You are likely to lose the full amount.

Cost of Learning Two Lessons

By doing so, at least you will learn two lessons. One is how to day trade. And the second is that perhaps day trading is not for you. There are a lot of people that have made a lot of money, but there's also a lot of people that you don't hear about that have lost a ton of money, as well. So don't get fooled and only listening to the good side, there is also a downside.

It would be very easy for anyone to tell you that, yes, you can make a lot of money doing this, and you will be more than fine.

But the reality is, a lot of that is just words. If this was very easy to be done, then everyone would be doing it. There's a lot of risks involved and it takes a lot of know-how, to ensure that you don't lose your investment.

There's a lot of risks involved with day trading. We do not recommend this strategy for the beginner.

Profits when Prices Rise or Fall

You can make profits when the stocks rise and you can make profits when the stock price falls.

To profit while the stock falls, the way to make a profit is you short the sale. What you do is instead of the normal process where you first you buy the shares and then you sell the shares. But in this case what you're doing is you're reversing the transaction so first, you sell the shares, and then you buy the shares. This is quite unusual. You are selling something that you do not own. There is a lot of risks involved with this transaction. So for example, if you strongly believe that the price of the stock for company XYZ is going to have a fall in share price, you might short the shares. The process would be to take 100 shares at $10 each and sell them, then buy them later at a bargain.

Shorting Shares
But you don't own them. That's fine. You're going to short them so what that means is you're going to first sell them. And then within a certain time frame, you must buy them.
Now the trick is within that time frame you want to make sure that the shares decrease in value.

So let's say you sold them at $10, and let's say you're able to buy the shares two days later, while the stock price falls to $5 and you're able to pick them up at $5. So now since you had 100 shares. You paid $5 a share so you paid, $500, and you received in revenues $1,000 which is hundred shares times $10. So you've made a profit of $500, and that's a very good result.

On the other hand, if this share price had increased dramatically. You could be in big trouble. Let's say instead of the price dropping to $5 it increased to $100. So now your revenues remain the same. You had 100 shares selling at $10, so your revenues were $1,000. Your cost now is $100 times 100 shares which is $10,000, which means you now have a loss of $9,000.

Limit your Risk
This is quite significant, especially when compared to the amount that you could earn. This is why it is important that when you short shares, you have to make sure that you have a stop-limit order so that you protect yourself from that stock growing too large and causing you some potential large losses. If you said that you're fine to lose $1 or $2 a share, what you could do is you could put a limit order at $12, meaning if the price picks up to $12, you would pick up 100 shares. Now if this were to occur, you would have picked up 100 shares at $12, and you would have 100 shares at $12, and you would have paid $1,200, This limited your loss to $200. So this is important to think about when you are doing day trading and especially when you're shorting shares because that's a very risky endeavor.

Before you start with day trading you must understand the risks that you're facing and you must understand the mechanisms that you can use to reduce the risk. You should also understand that each mechanism you use will come at a cost and that costs will reduce the amount of profits that you're going to earn, they could also increase your losses, despite this, they are necessary.

These are all the things you need to think about. You have to understand that the day traders are looking to make a small profit, every day and they understand that some days they will lose, and some days they will gain. But the idea is that they will gain on more days than they will lose.

Small Gains

Now what they might try to do is they would look to have very small gains perhaps about 0.5%. They are not looking for a 5% gain, they're looking to gain half a percent to 1% per day, or even less. So for example, if they have $10,000 that they're day trading, they're looking to make a gain of half a percent, that would be $50. But if you took this gain and you multiply that by five days a week that would be $250 a week, and then multiply that by 52 weeks that would be $10,000. In the year, over $10,000 with an investment of $10,000 that would be a 100% return. Now it's not very likely that people would win every day they're gonna have some days where they win and some days where they lose. So this difference between how many days you win and how many days you lose that will determine greatly your return on your investment.

The other thing you have to keep in mind is that there are fees when you invest, so each of these transactions will have certain fees that are costs, and if your fees are half a percent of the transaction. Then you have to make half a percent just to cover the fees and since there's a fee to purchase and a fee to sell. You have to make 1%, so you need to get your fees down to a minimum level. If you can get your fees down to 0.1%, then you can start making a profit with day trading. The lower your fees the better off you are. There's no reason to even try to start, day trading if you cannot get your fees lower than 0.5%.

If you get your fees down to 0.1% and you earn a 0.5% profit. Your real net profit is 0.3%, that's 0.5% minus two times 0.1%, because you got to pay 0.1% on the sale, and 0.1% on the buy. This leaves you with a profit of 0.3% and you can see that the fees have taken away a large part of your profits. Another way to reduce your fees is if you have flat fees, then you should have a large enough investment that the fees become negligible. If your fees are $5 per transaction and your investment is $5,000, then you are paying 0.1%, but if your investment is $50,000, now you are only paying 0.01%. This will have a very small effect on your results. It is important to keep in mind, that when you start, you should start with a very small investment, even if this means that you need to pay a higher percentage in fees. Do this, until you become an experienced day trader. It is better to pay a few extra fees than lose a $50,000 investment.

CHAPTER 10 - INVESTING FOR THE BEGINNER

"THE STOCK MARKET IS A DEVICE FOR TRANS-
FERRING MONEY FROM THE IMPATIENT TO THE
PATIENT." - WARREN BUFFETT

W hen you first start to invest, it is very common to not have a good understanding of all the terminology that is being used. This will make it very hard for the beginner to get ahead. Some very common terminology in investing that is used will sound difficult, complex, and hard to understand.

It is not Difficult
The reality is it's not that hard to understand and it's not that hard to make a profit in investing. Many people would like to maintain this idea that

it's very complex and only a few and only the wealthy people can do it. The reality is **anyone can succeed in investing and everyone should be doing it.** Once you understand that you can study for years and still be outperformed by the market then you can understand that it's really not about what you know but it's really about the strategies you that you use. There is not one person out there, perhaps with the exception of Warren Buffett and perhaps one or two others, that is capable of consistently outperforming the market. If there was a person that was able to get to 3% better than the market then that person would be a billionaire many times over. Many suggest that they can consistently outperform the market, if this were true, they would be billionaires.

An important thing to understand is that despite that there are hundreds and thousands of brokers very few of them earn more money then you would earn by just putting your money in the market or an ETF that follows the market. Think about what that means, this means despite years of training and years of work experience they're still not able to beat a person that simply invests in one ETF and holds them.

Brokers Underperform Compared to Market
Time after time, the stockbrokers have underperformed compared to the market. This means that you can also perform better than these stockbrokers by simply investing in the market and we

will show you how you can easily achieve this.

So before you invest in the market, must you know everything there is to know about stocks? **Absolutely, not.** You only need to know a few things and then you're ready to invest. Most people that just follow these simple rules that we will outline for you, and you will outperform those that spend years and years trying to digest knowledge trying to get a slight advantage. Many people are paid hundreds of thousand dollars per year that's simply do not outperform the market.

This means that despite their high salaries and despite the amount of work that they put in they still will be outperformed by the simple purchase of some ETFs. When you fully understand this concept you will understand that it is not rocket science and there's a lot of luck involved but you can get rid of the luck by basically investing in the long term. The goal here is not to invest in the short-term and not to become a day trader, at least for the beginner. If you want to beat the average stockbroker on Wall Street, all you have to do is follow the long term strategy and you will that may beat 80% of them or more.

ETF Strategy
To beat most of them, all you have to do is follow the ETF strategy that we outline for you. The main thing is to try to follow a long-term approach as opposed to a short-term approach. As well, do not

recommend that you try to follow trends, you should try to follow the opposite of a trend. When stocks are falling in price that's the time to start thinking about buying and when stocks are rising in price that's the time to start thinking about selling. What many individuals do is, as stocks start to rise in price they think that they should also take advantage of these rising prices. Then they buy that stock at a rather elevated price with the hope that it will go higher but there is a very equal chance that the prices will start to go down. What has occurred is people start to buy stocks at elevated prices and then it peaks and starts to fall. Many people will lose, as they bought while prices were rising and now prices will fall. The beginner investor should never follow trends. This is not a long term strategy. Beginners should stick with long term strategies that get results and are easy to follow with less risk. Following trends means as prices rise, this is when you buy and as prices fall, this is when you sell. This is exactly the opposite of what you want to be doing.

Your goal will be to do the opposite, when you see the stock prices to start to rise you should start thinking about selling. When you see that stock prices are starting to fall you should start thinking about buying. **This is how to succeed in stock markets and investing.**

The most important thing you need to know, as you may feel like you know very little about stocks and stock markets or the whole economy, is that by following some simple strategies, you can outperform most investors. The reality is that it may be very true, that you know a relatively small amount about stocks and investing, but you need to consider some people who have been studying this for years and know a lot more than you do, but they also do not get value from knowing that. **The vast majority of those same people that have studied this for years and have been working at it for decades will be outperformed by the market.**

What does is it mean to be outperformed by the market? This is a very common idea, the market performs every year in a certain way. Some years, the markets may rise and get great gains and returns, while other years they may decline and cause some losses. Being outperformed by the market, simply means that the market did better than your shares did. In essence, a stockbroker should meet the market. If you randomly held several stocks in the market, by random odds you should meet the market. But if you are buying and selling, then you may pay more fees and lose on some gains, this could cause you to be outperformed by the market. If you imagine the whole market moves in one general direction. Let's say the market has increased by 6% this year, so if you had invested in the whole market you would have increased by 6% if you underperform compared to the market you will have earned less than 6% so you may have earned 5%. This is a very important concept. The reason it is very important is it illustrates to you that even with all the studying in the world people are outperformed by the market. So no matter how much you study you have a good chance of being outperformed by the market. By understanding this concept, you understand that it is slightly a fool's errand to try to learn all that you can about the market and try to beat the market. You will be better off just trying to meet the market. You don't have to spend years in school and you don't even have to fully understand the stock market to meet the market. All you need to do is invest in that market with a few ETFs.

If someone asks you why you investing in this ETF and not investing in this mutual fund, you can simply say what was the performance of that mutual fund for the last 10 years and what fees did he or she end up paying. Most people may not even be able to answer that question even though they are the ones that are investing in those mutual funds. Many people invest in these funds because their stockbroker told them to invest in those funds. It may be the case, that the broker has the best of intentions for that client but at the end of the day most of these mutual funds will be outperformed by the market It is not to say that all of them will be, but the majority of them will be.

Success in Investing

When you understand this, you will understand that to be successful in the stock market you need to be investing in the long-term and you need to not worry about the trends, and you need not completely study every stock in the market.

To be successful you need to meet the market or exceed the market you don't want to be in a position where the market is getting more gains than you are gaining. It is very easy to meet the market all you need to do is invest in the market. So let's say you look at NASDAQ and you want to meet this market, which means that you will exceed most mutual funds that invest in NASDAQ all you have to do is invest in ETFs that follow NASDAQ. You will beat most mutual funds that are investing in NASDAQ and you will not have to work every day to do so. You will be participating in a passive fund as opposed to an active fund. The passive fund follows several rules and invests according to those rules and that's it. They don't study which stocks to buy and they don't study which stocks to sell. It just follows the simple principles of the market and invest to keep up with the market. The great thing with this approach is that the fees are low and the other great thing with this approach is that it doesn't take much to think about, it is very simple to apply. You also do not have that many transactions as you would in an active portfolio and this means you have a lot less fees. You also do not have to pay for a fund manager to focus on which stocks they should buy and which stocks they should sell. This is all done automatically.

Now, you have the strategy where you can beat 80% of the stockbrokers and mutual funds out there.

What about investing in individual stocks?

That is another question altogether and this strategy is worthwhile to consider. But in the beginning, it is far better to make sure that you meet the market and you can do so by following the ETF strategy.

Investing in individual stocks is a way for you to beat the market and that will be something that will be training you to do in phase 2. But in phase 1 the goal is to meet the market and this would beat 80% of the mutual funds. Most people can go their whole life being successful in phase 1 and never have to move to phase 2. With success in phase 1, you can increase your portfolio substantially. You can earn an investment return on average somewhere between 6% and 12% per annum, which is a great return. If you can invest $1,000 to $2,000 per month for the next 30 years then you can have a sizable portfolio at the end. You will be able to retire quite comfortably. The goal will be to be able to invest $2,000 per month and even $3,000 per month. You can start in the first few years with $1,000 a month, but you will need to increase this over time or take more years to build up a strong portfolio. We will show you how to do this and will have a calculator for you to estimate what your ending balance will be. Even if you start investing at $1,000, then change later to $2,000, and then even later to start investing at $3,000 per month and much more.

This is how you succeed at investing.

Perfect Phase 1 First
You first succeed in phase 1, which is investing with ETFs and meeting the market. Then you start to think about phase 2, and you start succeeding there. In phase 2, the goal will be to beat the market, as you are already meeting the market in Phase 1. Once you have success in both phase 1 and phase 2 you can determine how much of your investment you want to keep going in phase 1 and how much you want for phase 2.

The great thing about Phase 1 is that it is is very simple. Phase 2 is not quite as simple but it's not completely complex we will go over that later. We will talk about it in this book but our next book in this series will go into a lot more detail for Phase 2. The goal of Phase 2 is to even exceed the market, this will be accomplished through value investing, which is another long term investing approach.

The goal of this book is really to have beginners, who feel that they don't know how to invest, to gain the knowledge to be able to talk to their brokers and to know what questions to ask, and to be able to request the right stocks to purchase and more importantly the right ETF. Our goal is that the beginner can meet the market and succeed as well as most of the super-wealthy and perform even better.

The beginner investor must also understand that most people who talk about stocks do not know what they're talking about. They may have worked on wall street for 30 years and they may get a great salary but most people do not know how to invest properly, even the stock brokers. You can make a lot of money earning 5% to 6% per year and if you are earning this for your clients they will be generally quite happy. But they may not be as happy if they realize that if they had just invested in the market they could earn 8% to 10% per year. So this is the thing you should consider, what did I make and how much did the market make. Most people are very happy making 6%, but what if they understood that the whole market made 8%. Then, they lost 2% as an opportunity cost.

During one year a person's portfolio could increase by 10% and that person can be very proud and think that earning 10% in one year is a great result. It may sound great but then if you realize that the whole market increased by 15%, that person has underperformed compared to the market.

So don't just look at the value of the increase look at the value of the total increase in the market and then compare that to the value of the increase of that mutual fund or of that person's investment.

If someone is advising you to buy a mutual fund, then ask the person what was his rate of return over the past 15 years and how do they compare to the rate of return of the market. Then ask what are the fees involved per year. Ask if they can compare that to the return of NASDAQ or Berkshire Hathaway or S&P 500. You probably will not get a proper answer to this question. You're probably better off to do your own research here.

Stock Market is not a Science
This concept that we are talking about is the most important concept for a beginner to understand. The market is not a science it can act in some very strange ways. If you think about it, this is because people invest in very strange ways that it also acts in those strange ways. If everyone feels that a certain stock is now a stock that they're going to invest in, then that price will rise. It doesn't mean that the value of the company has increased it only means that people think it has more value. The prices will increase, this is an important concept to understand. Once you understand this then you have understood the main gist of what it

means to be an investor.

I know it seems counterintuitive and I can understand how it would seem that this cannot be correct but it is correct. Many people who have been investing for the past 40 years and have millions of dollars in their portfolio and they are not even aware of this concept. They feel that most stockbrokers would have some added information that they would know that they do not have. This is a crazy idea. But it is a prevalent idea also. Most people believe this and that feeds into the idea that you need to have a stockbroker to give you these recommendations. The most important take away from this chapter is that most stockbrokers, if not virtually all stockbrokers are not able to outperform the market. If you follow some very simple rules you can beat most of them and meet the market. These simple rules can be outlined in a few pages. If you follow the ETF strategy, you will beat most stockbrokers and meet the market.

The Bet
This may sound unbelievable and I agree that it sounds quite difficult to believe I can attest that it is true. I recommend that you look up Warren Buffett and his famous bet. In the following book in this series, we speak about this bet and how it explains exactly this topic. In short, Warren Buffett had a bet with some of his Wall Street colleagues that he could invest in the market and

that the market would outperform any of their active portfolios. This means that if you were to invest in an ETF or a passive fund, the passive fund would outperform any of their selected active funds. The bet essentially states that he bets that a fund that just follows simple rules and has no analysis will beat an active portfolio that buys and sells regularly. There were not many that took his bet, but some did. The bet was for $1 million to be donated to the charity of their choice. The bet was to run for 10 years and within a few years, it was very clear that Warren Buffett was going to win. This is proof of exactly what we are talking about, that despite many years of experience and all the education, most stockbrokers are not able to outperform the market.

Repeat this sentence and say it out loud **"most stockbrokers cannot outperform the market"**. You have now just learned more than most people who have been investing for decades. This is a critical thing for you to learn because what it's going to teach you is that there are going to be many people with decades of experience and degrees that are going to be telling you what you should invest in and you need to just say, no, I know what I'm going to invest in, and it is this list of ETFs.

They may even want to show you some of the mutual funds they would recommend, you should be very cautious about this. They may have your best interests at heart and they may feel that this is the best thing for you, remember most of the mutual funds are outperformed by the market. As well, unfortunately, many of the stockbrokers get fees in different ways depending on the type of funds they sell to their client. There have been situations where brokers would get increased fees for selling certain types of mutual funds. This should not be allowed, as it could affect the advice you are given. It is not to say that a broker will act against your best interest, but you should be aware that it is possible that a broker would get more commissions with certain types of invest-ments. This should never occur. The best thing to do is to invest in those ETFs that we recommend and have a consistent and long term strategy. If a broker is recommending you to go to another mu-tual fund, do your homework, check out the past 15 years of returns, and what is the expense ratio that you will be paying.

I would also advise you that you separate your investment advice from your broker. Meaning if you are to take investment advice from some-one it should be someone other than the person who is affecting your transactions. This way fees will not get in the way of a recommendation. You should also not be paying for recommendations, this should come free of charge.

To summarize what you have learned in this chap-ter is that investing is quite easy. You can beat most brokers. In fact, by the time you read this book, you will have enough information to beat most of the brokers on Wall Street and get a higher return rate than most investors. If a broker does give you information what you need to do is say thank you very much I'm going to look into that but do the transaction as you had planned and then say you going to look into that potential investment next month. Never take their advice before researching it on your own. This will give you a month to determine if it is the right fit for you. Then do the research and look at the fee structure if these fee structures are too high then do not buy this fund.

Earn more than Most

Now you know more than most investors and many investors that have been investing for decades with portfolios worth millions. You are ready to get higher returns than most of them.

CHAPTER 11
- MINDSET

"I MADE MY FIRST INVESTMENT AT AGE ELEVEN. I
WAS WASTING MY LIFE UNTIL THEN."

- WARREN BUFFET

Having the right mindset is very important for investing.

You do not want to be in a situation
where you're getting very emotional because the
stocks go up and down. The stocks will go up and
down every day and every week and every year,
what you need to do is avoid those ups and downs
and how it affects your emotions.

No Emotions
It is a normal feeling to want to get out of the

stock market when the prices fall. The minute you start seeing the stock market decline. You are losing money at this point. But what you need to do is get rid of those feelings. The worst thing that you can do is act on those feelings. So the normal feeling is 'oh I'm losing money, let me pull out' whatever you do, do not fall into this trap. So, when the stocks are at a lower price, this is exactly what you don't want to do if you did the exact opposite of this you would start to win. So if the whole market starts to decline, it is not the time to sell, but it is the time to buy.

Look at Declines as Opportunities

Keep this in mind when stocks go down. Don't look at this as a loss look at this as an opportunity. It is your opportunity to pick up deals and to pick up stocks at lower prices. The prices will increase. If you sell now what could happen is you could sell at a low price, and then two weeks later, the price goes up, and you've lost that whole gain.

If you had just stayed in, you would have gained. So do not sell at any time when there's a decrease.

If there's a significant increase then this is a time to think about selling, but not when you start losing money. Only when you start gaining money. For the beginner, it's a much better strategy to just stay in, when the stock markets decline. Buy and buy more. When the stock markets, increase, you can either sell a little, or perhaps buy a little less, but the best strategy and the simplest strategy is to keep buying as is. You need to make sure that you're making your monthly investment every month, do not skip out and do not put it aside. Remember, always pay yourself first. This means, put the funds into your investment account before you do anything else.

When Markets Rise

If the stock markets increase, well your portfolio has just risen. So all the more reason to buy stocks. If the stock markets decrease, well now the prices are at a better deal. So all the more reason to buy. If there's a year or two years of a bear market, then that's a good time to start investing and to keep on investing, because sooner or later, it will turn into a bull market, and the prices will start to go up. If you look at the stock prices over the last 100 years, you will see that the stock prices have always been increasing. So keep this in mind when you're investing, if you're investing for the long term. You will always have a gain if you look at any 20 year period or more. The stock market was higher at the end than at the beginning during any 20 year period. So this is why you should be looking at a minimum of 20 years to invest. And you should be investing equally during those 20 years.

You could have a smaller investment window, perhaps over five years, but at least what you need to do is don't invest at all in one month, because that way you could invest when stocks are overpriced, this will harm your overall return rate, in the long run.

Phase Your Entry

The challenge with investing a large amount in a short period is that if the stocks are overvalued, then you will pay a higher price than the value you get. If you invest over five to ten years, you will minimize this risk.

So keep this in mind, and follow the strategy and you will do well.

Mindset is Key

Remember, your mindset is key. Do not look at negatives, as a negative, look at them as an opportunity. So if the stock market decreases, yes your portfolio has gone down. Yes, perhaps you have lost some money in that period. But as well, look at this as an opportunity. It is now time to buy even more stocks at these lower prices. Remember you are investing for the long term. You are an investor you are not a day trader and you're not even a trader. So what does that mean? You're investing for 10, 20, 30 years or longer which means whatever stock you buy you will not sell it for the next 10 or 20 years unless there's some remarkable event that was to occur. So for example, if the whole stock market increased by 30%, then that might be a time to consider whether you should sell off a portion of that. But for now, this is very unlikely. And for now, just keep investing and keep investing over a consistent period, and do not act emotionally, one way or the other. If you are unsure, then do not sell. If you feel the prices are going down, then do not sell.

Opposite of the Trend

Warren Buffett famously said that it is best to be greedy when others are fearful and be fearful when others are greedy. What he means by this is when people are starting to buy actively the prices will go up. This is the time to be fearful, and by being fearful that it's the time to think about selling, and not the time to be buying. On the other hand, when people are fearful they end up selling the prices will start to drop. This is the time not to fall into that fear and follow those people, but rather to follow your strategy and have the idea that the stock market is now cheaper and there are more deals today than there was yesterday. So keep this in mind, do not sell just because everyone's selling, and do not buy just because everyone's buying, do not follow the trends. And do not get emotional with investing. If for some reason you're questioning whether your investment a few weeks ago or a few months ago was right or wrong. Don't do that.

Long Term

Remember you are investing for the long term and not the short term.

If you want to question things, then wait three to

five years and start to look at how your markets are going, but do not do this after two or three months, especially when you are following the ETF strategy.

CHAPTER 12
- DON'T TAKE
ADVICE FROM
STOCKBROKERS

"THE STOCK MARKET IS FILLED WITH INDIVIDUALS
WHO KNOW THE PRICE OF EVERYTHING, BUT THE
VALUE OF NOTHING."

- PHILLIP FISHER

This may sound counterintuitive, but most stockbrokers don't know what they're talking about. And most of their advice will be completely irrelevant to you. I was thinking to title this chapter originally stockbrokers don't know shit.

But I thought that might be a little bit too harsh. I use these very strong words to drive the point. They really do know a lot, but you do not need to know a lot to beat the market.

So I decided to call it, don't take the advice of stockbrokers.

But the reality is, the takeaway message for this chapter is stockbrokers don't know shit. Now it seems a bit much to be saying that. How can I say that, so strongly?

But the reality is that most stockbrokers are beaten by the market. So what does that mean? It means that if you just take a random market, and invest in the market.

You will beat at least 80% of the stockbrokers. That means basically if you do no homework, no research, and just invest in any market. You will beat 80% of them.

When you think about this. It is saying that the best-studied chess player in the world could be beaten by a child.

Because the reality is you do not need any information to invest in the market. All you need to know is which stocks to invest in, follow the market, and that can take you all of five minutes to research, or we can give it to you in this book. And by doing that you will beat 80% of the stockbrokers. So yeah, it's not too outlandish to say stockbrokers don't know shit.

Not Hard to Outperform

When in fact a child can beat 80% of the stock market. You could show a child six stocks and ask him or her to pick one of them but each of those stocks follows a market. Then what will happen is that child will pick one or two or three or four, and they will beat 80% of the stockbrokers in that market. If you pick the New York Stock Exchange, or NASDAQ or S&P 500 you will beat the vast majority of all stockbrokers on Wall Street when you invest in an ETF geared for these markets. When you can say a child can beat most stockbrokers on Wall Street, then it's not too far of a leap to say stockbrokers don't know that much.

This is very important for you to understand. Most brokers would like to show a return within the year, this tends to make them shorter-term investors, but longer-term investors do better. This is part of the issue, the other issue is that with so many transactions, there is a slight cost to each and as well, they could be losing slightly on each trade.

Once you understand this, then you can understand that the strategy you're following will beat 80% of the stockbroker's advice. Not only that, but it will also be a significant portion of the people investing. Because Don't forget those top brokers are getting paid to advise investors. So the investors are following those stockbrokers and those investors are earning less money, so you will have a great advantage because you will not be following their advice. After all, you know the magic words, you know, that stockbrokers don't know shit. Again, we are being purposely extreme so that you get the point. Take the investment advice you receive from an investor with a grain of salt.

Information and Training
With little information and little time spent practicing and you will be able to beat 80% of them, and also able to beat most of the people who are investing.

This secret alone is worth the cost of this book, and probably 200 times the cost of this book. It is also a secret I wish I had known when I was starting out investing because I did not know this. I was not aware that stockbrokers don't know that much.

If I was aware of that, then I would have chosen different strategies. During my first five years of investing I did pretty poorly because I followed a lot of the advice of the stockbrokers, and it's something that I would not have done today. I did all the beginner mistakes. I became very emotional about investing. That's a very beginner move you cannot do that. I also made the mistake of listening to advice from friends and also listening to advice from brokers. This proved to be the wrong advice, I also listened to my brokers who were sort of pushing a certain amount of mutual funds. Well, those mutual funds were very expensive and they were underperforming compared to the market. So I was losing on two fronts. Yes, I was making a little bit of revenue, but not the revenue that I should be making.

This chapter is important for you to understand that there's going to be a lot of people telling you this and that. But the basic thing is, if they do not understand ETFs, and if they do not understand the difference between a mutual fund and the difference between an ETF, and a passive investment versus active investment, then please do not listen to them.

Thank them for their information, you may tell them that in your view, you believe that the ETF is a better strategy. Listen to what they have to say, but don't let them convince you of something different to the ETF strategy.

Other Strategies
If someone is really promoting something as a different strategy to the ETF and that starts to make sense, feel free to contact us and we will listen to what you have to say. And let you know if you're on the right track or not.

If there is a better strategy out there for beginners, we'd love to hear it but the honest to goodness truth is there is not a better strategy for a beginner. I've seen many strategies and this is the only strategy that beats 80% of the mutual funds and beats most long term strategies and for sure beats any kind of day trading strategy.

The only strategy that can compete with this strategy is called value investing. And that's another strategy that we recommend, but we recommend that in phase two. So the first thing we recommend for you is to get good with the ETF strategy and use that for the bulk of your portfolio until you can get to the point where your value investing strategy exceeds your ETF strategy.

Hard to beat the ETF Strategy
In terms of performance, it is important to note that the ETF strategy takes almost no time at all. Whereas the value investing strategy which is also a very good strategy does take some time and some research and evaluation. Knowing what your goals are and knowing what you're trying to do is important. If you're fine with earning an 8% to 12% return, which is far better than most mutual funds, then go for it. Now remember there are going to be mutual funds that are doing even higher returns in year one and even for a few years, but what you got to look at is the long term outlook. If they have a history of two years of very good returns, then start looking elsewhere.

If they're an active portfolio, start looking elsewhere. This is important to understand, the concepts here are very simple the ETF strategy will beat every strategy out there, except the strategy of value investing, which takes more time, more understanding and more risk. But for a beginner, we do not recommend you start with value investing we recommend you start with the ETF strategy, and it will beat over 80% of the stockbrokers that will try to tell you something else.

People are people and they want to believe that they're doing their job well, a stockbroker is never going to admit to you that a child can beat them at their job. Well, the reality is most children can beat most stockbrokers, it's a sad thing to say, but it's honest to goodness truth, all you have to do is train the kid to choose one of the ETFs, and they can beat the majority of the stockbrokers. So a child can follow this strategy you can have them pick one of four cards each month, each representing one of our recommended ETFs, and this strategy will beat most stockbrokers.

Keep that in mind when you're investing and understand this point, and you will succeed in your investment. I see many people, many millionaires, many businessmen, who say, I need to speak with my broker I have to see what he says about this. The reality is that the broker knows, next to nothing about what the future will be. And if he did know that much, that stockbroker would not be working with a multimillionaire that stockbroker would be working with the likes of Bill Gates, Jeff Bezos, and Warren Buffett.

It may sound very extreme to say that a stockbroker knows very little. The reality is they know a lot and have worked very hard to gain that knowledge, but the reality is with all that knowledge and training, this does not generally result in better results. It is not the fault of the stockbroker, it is the fact that the stock market is an imperfect system. However, if you follow some simple rules, you will beat most investors. Invest in passive index funds or ETFs and hold for the long term. Following this strategy you will beat most advice from most stockbrokers.

You should, however, speak with a professional about investing, but just make sure that you take their advice with a grain of salt and do your own homework as well.

CHAPTER 13 - TERMINOLOGY

"ONE OF THE FUNNY THINGS ABOUT THE STOCK MARKET IS THAT EVERY TIME ONE PERSON BUYS, ANOTHER SELLS, AND BOTH THINK THEY ARE ASTUTE."

- WILLIAM FEATHER

It is critical to get a good understanding of all the terminology commonly used in investing. There are many more terms, but these are the terms that you will need to understand for the beginner investor. You must understand that even the beginner investor can earn a great livelihood as an investor. More importantly, most investors that have earned millions of dollars in the stock market do not even understand the basics. By understanding the terminology used in this chapter you will surpass most casual investors and many investors that have been earning millions of dollars and some earning tens of millions over their investing careers.

Asset Allocation - this is how much you have invested in cash, bonds, and stocks.

Asset, something that can earn future revenue for you. It is something that you own and you control and it has the potential to be of future value, generally in the form of generating a revenue stream for you. Stocks can fall into this category, as they would generate dividend income for you. Rental properties also is an asset, as you would derive rental income. Bonds also fall into this category, as you derive interest income. Hence, stocks, bonds, and rental properties all fall under the category of assets.

Balance Sheet is the financial statement that shows the amount of assets, liabilities, and equity that a company has at a specific point in time, usually at the year-end.

Income Statement, this is the financial statement that shows the financial operations of a company during a period. It would show all the revenues and all the expenses, the difference would show up as a profit or loss. This statement can also be called the P&L statement, or the profit and loss statement. They are used interchangeably. The income statement is generally for one year. The income statement is very important to understand how profitable a company is or can be. It will be the critical report to use when looking at value investing.

Financial Reports, the financial reports of a company is generally the complete set of financial reports for the company. The two most important financial statements are the balance sheet and income statement. You also have the Cash Flow statement or statement of changes in financial position.

Bear Market is a market that has a downward trend and the belief is that the trend will continue. If you believe the market will drop, you could be called a bear or you could be called "bearish". This is not a negative word, it is just a word to describe your belief that the trend will be negative. A bear market can last for days, weeks, months, and even years.

Bull Market is a market that is generally increasing. The bull is a sign that things are going well. The famous symbol of Wall Street is the statue of the bull. Someone who believes the markets will improve can be called a bull or can be called "bullish".

Broker, this is the person or entity that buys and sells on your behalf. You cannot buy or sell stocks directly, you must have an entity do it on your behalf. You pay fees for this service. The service can be a flat fee or as a commission on the sale or purchase. Other brokers that manage your fund can charge a percentage of your total portfolio.

Diversified Portfolio, this means that you are buying many stocks and stocks in many industries, this way you are reducing your risk. There is risk involved when you put all of your eggs in one basket, by diversifying your portfolio, you are reducing this risk.

Hedge Fund - an entity that is set up to invest by the hedge fund manager or the money manager. This entity will receive investments and then the money manager will invest with those investments with the idea of getting a good return for their investors. This can be risky but it also can result in some good returns.

Margin - This is essentially a loan from your broker that would allow you to purchase more shares. It comes with risk, but it is a way for you to invest in more shares than the money you have in the account.

Margin Call - this is where the prices of the stocks have decreased so much that your margins are no longer supported by the cash in your investments. You would need to make this margin call or potentially lose your complete investment.

Risk/reward - there is a concept that when you have no risk you get no reward and the higher your risk the higher your reward. For the most part, this is true, but beware of situations where the risk is high but the reward is low. Your goal will be to find those areas of high reward with low risk.

Bonds - a bond is a loan that you are giving to a company. It is relatively low risk when dealing with companies that have a good going concern. The basic thing about a bond is that you know what your return will be. When the bonds come due, you would collect your investment back and you would earn interest as well.

Stocks and Shares - stocks of a company is owning a very small share of that company. If a company has one million shares outstanding and you purchase one of those stocks, you own one-millionth of that company. It is a very small slice, but it is a slice nonetheless. You would then earn that share of the company's profits. The reason the terms are used interchangeably is that one stock is the lowest share of a company that you can purchase. One stock equals one share of that company.

Expense Ratio - this is the amount of fees that you will be paying in fees to manage a mutual fund. These change from fund to fund, but they average slightly above 1%, their range can be from 0.5% to 2% or higher, depending on the fund. The unfortunate thing about an expense ratio is that it lowers the rate of your return.

Index, is a collection of stocks or assets that are

used as a benchmark to track results. S&P 500 is an example of an index. The goal of an index is generally to set a benchmark. You can compare your results to the results of that index.

Index Funds, is a specific type of mutual fund, that follows a specific index. It is a passive investment because it follows a specific market without the intention of trying to beat that market. As such, it also has lower fees.

Exchange-Traded Funds (ETF), are very similar to mutual funds but they are listed on exchanges and you can purchase them just like stocks. They also follow an index and are passive investments with low fees.

EPS or earnings per share, this is the value of taking the current earnings and dividing it by the number of shares outstanding. Hence, if a company has earned $10 M in the past year, and they have 10 million shares outstanding, this would result in the following calculation $10 M/ 10 M, which is $1 per share. It would then have an EPS of $1.

PE ratio, the price-earnings ratio is the division of the trading price by the EPS. Hence, if a share is trading at $60 and it has an EPS of $3, then it would have a PE ratio of 20.

Ask - the lowest price that a seller is willing to sell.

Market Cap - this is calculated by multiplying the current trading price by the number of shares outstanding. In a way, it is the valuation of the company that the market gives to the company. If the shares have a price of $100 per share and 10 million shares are outstanding, this would give a market cap of $1 B, which is $100 multiplied by 10 million.

Prospectus - this is the collection of information that an investor needs to determine if they should invest or not. It is not the complete list but it is a great starting point. You then need to do your own research on top of the prospectus. Do not think that having the prospectus is sufficient, it is only the starting point.

NASDAQ, (National Association of Securities Dealers Automated Quotations), which is broken down to give NASDAQ. It is a U.S. exchange that trades in securities, which is based in New York. There is an index for this called Nasdaq. This was founded on February 4, 1971. It has approximately 3,500 listings with a total market cap of $10 trillion.

S&P 500, the S&P is derived from Standard and Poor's, the 500 is the number of companies that are in this index. It was founded on March 5, 1957. It is one of the most commonly founded indexes and a very good one, as it has a significant number of very large companies. It has a total market cap of over $20 trillion.

Dow Jones or the Dow Jones Industrial Average is a list of the top 30 large companies found within the NYSE and the S&P 500. There is a lot of over-lap between the Dow Jones, the NYSE, and the S&P 500. Generally, when one does well, so do the others. It is important to note that the Dow only has 30 companies, while the S&P 500 has 500 or more. The Dow Jones Industrial Average began on May 26, 1896. The Dow Jones was created by Charles Dow and Edward Jones.

New York Stock Exchange (NYSE) and also called the Big Board, is an American stock exchange lo-cated on Wall Street. It is the largest Stock Ex-change in the world by far. It has over 2,400 listing which makes it almost five times larger than the S&P 500.

CHAPTER 14 - INTEREST RATES AND THE FED

"WHEN EVERYTHING SEEMS TO BE GOING AGAINST YOU, REMEMBER THAT THE AIRPLANE TAKES OFF AGAINST THE WIND, NOT WITH IT."

– HENRY FORD

Interest rates play a big role in investing. When the interest rates are higher, people will shift from investing in stocks and look to invest in bonds or term deposits. They will focus more on earning interest than on earning dividends or gains on sales. While if the interest rate decreases then this shifts the other way.

This factor is important due to supply and demand. If you increase the demand but keep the same supply then price increases, while if you decrease demand but keep the same supply then price decreases.

Investors should understand this basic principle. Also, as interest rates fall it becomes cheaper for companies to get access to cheaper loans and thus provide more income to shareholders by increasing their debt to equity ratio. This will also have the effect of increasing stock prices. Hence, a decrease in interest rates causes two reasons for an increase in share prices. While an interest rate increase will cause a two reasons for a decrease in stock prices.

It is important to keep ahead of what the interest rates will do.

For the past many years, the rates have been very low. It is likely to stay this way. There has been a drive to keep stock prices higher. The challenge here is that the interest rates cannot get any lower. They are basically as low as you can get right now.

The Fed

The Fed sets the rates for interest rates in the United States. The Fed is related but separate from the government. If you can predict what the Fed will do, this can help with your investing strategy. Right now, it is difficult to say when the Fed will increase the rates. What conditions would cause a rise in interest rates? If there is a period of high inflation, then this is a good time to increase the interest rates, but there have not been periods of high inflation for quite some time.

Inflation may be one of the best indicators of when there will be an interest rate hike, but it is not likely to occur for some time. The conditions would need to exist for that to occur. There would need to be more demand than supply. The problem is to get more demand, you would need wages to go up in the United States. Wages have not really increased that significantly in years. Hence, this is not likely. You could also get more people with the same wages, in other words, increase the population, but this also seems to be quite stagnant and this takes generations to change. Hence, do not expect great growth here.

Globalization
The fact that the market is becoming more globalized can help with increasing demand but not for all products, just for those that are offered on the global market. It also means facing global competition. Hence, some industries can benefit and other industries could pay a price.

When looking at all of these factors, it is not very likely that there will be a big change when it comes to the Fed rate or interest rate in general. This is a positive sign it means that stock prices will not be negatively affected by this change. On the other hand, the only way the Fed can change the rates is a Fed rate hike. Keep that in mind too.

The increase in interest rates is also a political decision. In politics high stock prices are equivalent to success, hence, it is unlikely that a new government would like to increase interest rates and cause a drop in stock prices. It is difficult to imagine a time where a president would like to increase the interest rate knowing that it will cause a decrease in stock prices.

It is very likely that we will see low-interest rates for the next long while.

With this in mind, it should affect how much you have of interest-bearing investments versus other investments. When interest rates are lower, you would need to decrease the percentage of interest-bearing investments and move those investments into stocks, real estate, or both.

When interest rates drop, this is a great benefit to the real estate market, as you will be able to pay less on your mortgages. You will still pay the same capital amount, but you will pay far less in interest. This is particularly true if you have a long term mortgage, of 20 years or more.

As interest rates drop, the demand for real estate and stocks go up and the demand for interest-bearing investments go down. While the opposite is true when interest rates increase.

This will not play a factor in your day to day investing activities, but it is important to understand the effect of the Fed's interest rate hikes or decreases on the stock prices and effects on real estate. If there is a hike, then stock market prices will go down. This may sound like a negative effect. In the short run, it will be negative, as your portfolio will have less value, but in the long run, it also gives an opportunity. It will mean cheaper prices and more deals for you to take advantage of.

It is important to look at every decrease in the market as an opportunity and not a loss. Also keep in mind that for all decreases in market prices, the prices have bounced back over a number of years and to a much greater extent. As a result, if you take advantage of these stock prices declines or market declines by investing more as they decline, then you will benefit from this. This approach works on the market as a whole but does not work on each individual share. A stock that is decreasing can go bankrupt and if you put all of your eggs in that one basket, then you could lose your total portfolio. When you are investing more as the market takes hits, it should only be on the market and not individual shares. In other words, you need to maintain a balanced and diversified portfolio. If you have 100 stocks, and they are in many diverse industries, then you are well diversified, but if 25% of your portfolio comes from one stock, then you are no longer well diversified since

25% of your portfolio is in one company. Ideally, you would have no more than 5% in one company to maintain a strong diversification and a goal would be to have no more than 2%, as well.

Keep in mind the effects of interest rates on your portfolio and your asset allocation. When the interest rates are increased, this could be an opportunity to purchase more stocks as the prices fall, but it is also a time to look at more real estate. This is the time to start using any reserves in cash that you have.

CHAPTER 15
- AUTOMATIC
SCREENERS

This is a way for you to find good potential stocks to invest in. It is important to understand that this strategy follows a more advanced strategy. But you need to know that these screeners are available.

The screener allows you to quickly determine what are your metrics or which types of stocks you are looking for and then this will find these stocks for you. It will save you hours of research on having to go through all the stocks to find the relevant ones.

For example, let's say that you are interested in stocks that have a price of somewhere between $10 and $50. You can enter that in and find these. You can also lookup all those that have a PE ratio of more than 10 or less than 50. You may want to find those that are trading at less than 200% of book value. Whatever you would like you can enter it here. These screeners will return the exact stocks that you are looking for.

There are also some predefined screeners that you can also use. You can find stocks that are paying dividends or those that are paying an increased amount of dividends. This tool allows you to improve your research time greatly.

This is only a tool, to find a list of stocks that may be of interest to you. You should still do your research on every stock that you decide you may want to invest in. There are also areas that you need to be aware of. The PE ratio may be lower due to a very high level of earnings in the past year, which is not expected to continue. This would result in a low PE ratio. So you need to do the full research. The tool is only a convenient tool to get a smaller list of stocks to focus on. Then you would need to do the full research on these stocks before you purchase.

This strategy is more advanced as you are not

investing in an ETF, but rather you are investing in individual stocks with this approach. As such, you should follow the value investing approach. Hence, this research will allow you to narrow down your research and focus on those stocks that you feel have great potential.

Then, when you do your valuations, you can decide when to purchase and when to sell. As discussed, in the chapter on value investing, once you have calculated an intrinsic value for your stock. Then you can set up a purchase price and a sales price. You could say that you will buy once the stock is selling below 25% of the value price or intrinsic price. You will sell once the shares are trading at 25% or 30% above the value price or intrinsic price. Hence, if you estimate the value to be $10, then you may not purchase until the share price is trading at $7.50 or below and you would not sell until the trading prices are at $12.50 and above. It is important to keep revaluing the value of the shares as after time, these valuations can change. They can increase and they can also go down.

The triggers to buy can be caused by the market or caused by increases or decreases in valuation.

The screener is a tool to do your initial research, it is not a tool to determine which stocks you should buy. This needs to be understood. It is also a tool that should be used as part of the value approach and only in the area of finding new stocks to value. If you find several great stocks in the screeners' tools, but they do not meet your valuation requirements or the valuation methods determine that you should not buy, then do not buy. Ultimately, the screener tool can be used as an adjunct to the valuation approach, but it can never be used instead of the valuation strategy.

The tool can only help you find stocks that you can start researching. You should have multiple ways of finding stocks that you can research, a screener tool should only be one of the methods to find potential companies, and the stocks that you research should not all come from one source.

Another great way is to look at stocks that Warren Buffett invests in. These should be added to your list of stocks that you research and you should find valuations for these. You can add some stocks from screeners, as well.

For a list of screeners that we recommend, see our website to get some high potential screeners. It is important to use this tool properly, it is not a tool to determine which stocks you should buy, it is only a tool to determine which stocks you should consider analyzing. There are hundreds of companies to choose from, you need to find a way to narrow down this list.

CHAPTER 16
- ARTIFICIAL
INTELLIGENCE
AND INVESTING

"THE WISE MAN PUT ALL HIS EGGS IN ONE BASKET
AND WATCHES THE BASKET."

– ANDREW CARNEGIE

A rtificial Intelligence will become a very important part of everyday life, and it is getting more important, each day and every day that passes.

How can we take advantage of artificial intelligence in the investing world?

The answer is that we can start programming

tools that can look at stocks and find out which stocks to invest and this can become a very powerful tool. If you think about it, a few decades ago, it was quite unusual to think that a computer could beat a man in chess.

Computerized Chess

When the first computerized chess games came out, they were quite simplistic and very easy to beat. I was able to beat them at the highest level and I'm a decent player at chess but I'm not a chess master.

So what happened? Well, computers got stronger and programmers got better and artificial intelligence started to work more and more. Computers, now, were able to teach themselves.

The best Go player in the world recently retired. And what he said was, there was no way that he could beat Google Go. So he gave up, this may seem like a trivial thing. But if you're the best player at Go in the world, and you cannot beat a computerized version of the game, then it is quite demoralizing for the best player in the world.

So he's simply retired from the game.

And I can understand him.

Artificial Intelligence

So the future for AI in investing can be quite similar.

When if all of a sudden, the stockbrokers are suddenly replaced by more and more computerized versions of the best chess player in the world, or the best Go player in the world.

This is already starting to happen and I think it's really important that you get in early on at the onset. But it's also important to look at what strategies are developed for each of the different programs that you can buy some strategies may be for day trading and some strategies may be for long term holding the strategies for day trading would be a lot riskier. And don't forget, the computer will need to calculate what people will do, which is not scientific.

It is not easy for a computer to figure out what humans will do.

Although one needs to think about if there are more and more computers in this market, then it will be a lot easier to figure out what computers would do, as opposed to what humans will do.

So this is a glimpse into the future and it's important to be aware of this happening and what you can do to take advantage of this.

It is not here completely yet. Although there are a few places where you can invest your stocks in a market that is handled by a computer. But currently, I would not advise you to do this, there's a lot of risks. It's better to speak to a broker and talk about a specific investment that's run by artificial intelligence.

But it's important to note that it is very likely that artificial intelligence will play a much stronger role in the years to come.

Future of Investing
And it may be not too far off, where the vast majority of stockbrokers are run by computers and not by individuals.

We would probably be looking at a 20 year period, at a minimum, before this changes.

So it's a good idea to get in on the ground, and to get a head start and to understand that this is coming. But understand it's still in the very basic years, and it's probably 20 years away from being very productive, but with technology, it's very hard to predict how fast things will move and tweaks can quickly change that makes what was expected to take five years to instead take five months.

So definitely get in on the start and definitely get ahead, start today and we will send you some lists of good starting points to start with this type of investment but remember it is highly risky and understand what the goals are before you get in.

Currently, there are no artificial intelligence brokers, that can beat the market. But who knows, years from now that could be very different. So just keep ahead of the curve and keep a lookout on this improvement on this front.

It is definitely an exciting area and potentially could make investing that much easier and less risky, although, it is not likely to occur within the next ten to twenty years. It is much like the advancement of AI, it advances every day, but it is not here yet, at least in a traditional sense.

CHAPTER 17 - AREAS TO WATCH

"STOP TRYING TO PREDICT THE DIRECTION OF THE STOCK MARKET, THE ECONOMY OR THE ELECTIONS." – WARREN BUFFETT

Some areas to watch out for, for the beginner. When you're a beginner and starting to invest, there are certain areas that you must be very aware of. The first thing is you will not have your confidence and that's okay. Do not allow this lack of confidence to affect your investing. The first thing you need to avoid is to make sure that you do not follow trends, you may see one stock rise and you see another stock fall, and you may want to get in on the trend do not do that. That is not for the beginner investor and that's not for any investor, following trends is a recipe for disaster.

Be the Tortoise

You may have a friend who says, Oh, I just made 10% on this one stock and in one day. Well, congratulate him and move on, your goal is not to go for the day trader and your goal is not to win in the short one. Your goal right now is to be the tortoise, not the hare. You can do a lot better by being the tortoise than being the hare. Warren Buffett would be a prime example of the tortoise winning compared to all of the hares. He is in it for the long term, not the short term, and he is showing exactly how it can be done and how the strategy can pay off. He did not win overnight and he never acted as a good day trader, and he is vehemently against following any trends and rightfully so. Those are some of the areas to watch out for the beginner do not follow any trends, do not follow the stocks so closely. If you're a beginner you should not be following these stocks daily, you should be just investing religiously as you are planning to do, and invest in those ETFs that suits your needs. For the beginner, your first strategy is to get good with the ETF strategy and this should be the bulk of your strategy for the rest of your life. You can dabble into other strategies, but only when you can show that you can get them to work on dummy accounts. And then, with a small sum of funds, and then you can start incrementing your investment size, but it is very unlikely that with any other strategy you will be able to get a result that is greater than the strategy you're getting with the ETF strategy. So keep that in mind.

Emotions and Investing do not Mix

The other thing is don't get nervous, you might see the stock going down, and the nervous reaction might be, oh I'm losing money, let me pull out to minimize my losses. Do not do this. This is a beginner move, and it will cost you dearly. When the stocks go down it's not a time to sell. If you sell, when the stocks go down you lose money. The right strategy is when the stocks go down significantly, you start to invest more, and you might even consider investing significantly more. This is the only time you can consider adjusting your strategy even slightly. What you could do is if the markets go down, slightly increase your monthly investment. Then the next month if they go down more than slightly increase some more. So this is a wise, time to have a little bit of side money that you can dip into to increase your investments when the stocks go down.

Modifying Investment Size

If you follow this strategy of increasing the amount of your monthly investment as stocks go down and conversely, decreasing, slightly as stocks rise, you will be following a winning principle, because you will get more stocks at lower prices and buy fewer stocks at higher prices, but just be aware that stocks will rise generally in prices. So if they rise 1% in a month. Do not adjust your buys, but if they rise 3% in that one month, then maybe it's time to consider purchasing slightly less. This is a strategy that you can use and you can play around with. But for the most part, you should be following, at least, 100% investment, each month so if your goal is to spend $24,000 a year investing. Your goal should be to split this up to $2,000 per month. You might want to adjust that slightly for price increases and dips, the range could be from $1,700 to $2,500, depending on how much the stocks have gone up or how much the stocks have gone down, but do not make the difference from zero investing, and $4,000, investing that range is too high. So keep this in mind and you will do well.

If you do not understand the advantage of increasing when stocks go down or decreasing when stocks go up, this is fine. The idea here is basically that as the stocks go down if you buy a little bit more than your prices will be a little bit lower on average, as stocks go up, if you buy a little bit less then your stock price average will also be a little less and you will make more money in the long run, but keep this with a grain of salt, and do not adjust your spend that much.

If you're going to adjust your strategy with this only adjust it by a maximum of 15% of your spend. So this way you're always a minimum investing at 85% if your average and maximum investing at 115% of your average. This way you can slightly increase your investment and get a slightly better result when you're using the ETF strategy.

But, even for this strategy we do not recommend this strategy for the beginner for the very beginner just follow the $2,000 per month strategy and keep this up, and within 30 to 40 years you'll be ready to retire. That's all you need to do, nothing more and nothing less.

Advice from Friends

The other thing you need to do is make sure that you do not follow advice from your friends.With regards to our friends, you do not know what is their investing career and they might have the right advice or they might not. So, the best thing to do is keep it in mind but keep with your strategy. If their strategy differs from your ETF strategy, do not use it. Never follow advice, if you do not understand the rationale of that advice or what strategy it is using for the long run.

Day Trading

Never get into day trading as a beginner, and never get into day trading before practicing it out on the dummy account. Once you've proven success on a dummy account for a minimum of six months to 12 months, then you can go to the next stage where you would only invest a minimum amount of real funds that you can be fine with losing. So for example, if you're investing $2,000 per month or $24,000 per year. Then you want to look at a maximum investment of one month. You could take one month and say, okay it's fine if I lose $2,000 and use that money to learn how to do day trading. But you gotta understand that you are very likely to lose the whole amount. If you want to learn day trading, you need to start with a sum that you are fine with losing completely. You can take this $2,000 as a cost to learn, day trading.

If you aren't successful and then continue with day trading. If you are not successful, consider that loss of $2,000 as two things. The first is the cost of learning how to day trade, and the second is the lesson that you should not be day trading that $2,000 is money well spent. You have learned how to day trade, and you've learned that day trading is not for you. This lesson could be far more costly than $2,000, so keep that in mind.

Do not follow the Charts

Also to not spend too much time looking at results, especially in the early years, you should be spending a few minutes a month, and no more. If you're looking at your portfolio, every day, then you're not doing it correctly. Because you are a long term trader and not a short term trader, therefore you should not be looking at the portfolio results, each month. At a maximum, you should be looking at them once per year, or perhaps even twice per year. But generally, you need to understand that you're investing for the long term, and there are certain periods where you will earn and there are certain periods where you will lose, and even years where you will lose, but that's fine. You're gonna have those years where your whole portfolio declines. So keep this in mind, and do not follow the stock market so closely. This will only cause you some panic and you will lose your valuable time.

Focus on Simple Strategies First
You need to follow the beginner strategies, and nothing else. Once you get good at the beginner strategies, then you can move on to more advanced strategies. Then you can start following those more advanced strategies, but not before you, you perfect the beginner strategy. So the first strategy you should be working on is the ETF strategy once you get that down, then you can start with the other strategies. So, aim to at least have a year or two years with the ETF strategy alone, and then start looking at other strategies. The next strategy that we advise you work on after the ETF strategy is the value investing strategy.

THANKS!

Thank you for taking the time to read this book. We hope that you enjoyed it and have learned a lot!

We would love to hear your feedback, both positive and constructive.

We would love to hear your feedback, you can do so by go to the following address:

https://markgruner.com/contact-us/feedback

BOOKS IN THIS SERIES

Investing for Beginners

Intensive training for beginners in investing. The goal of this series is to have people who know very little about investing, start to learn from day 1 and start to earn as well. With this four book series, you will learn the basics of investing and how to make your first investment. We will show you how to set goals and follow simple strategies that work.

You will beat most of the other investors out there by simply following our rules and being patient. We will go into more advanced strategies such as value investing and day trading.

By the end of this series, you will be no longer a beginner and you will be making money on your investments.

The Beginner's Guidebook To Invest-

ing

Warren Buffett Investment Strategies

A Begginer's Guide To Day Trading

The Beginners Guide To Options

BOOKS BY THIS AUTHOR

Money Matters For Personal Finance

No matter your financial situation - improve it! This book will show you how to save on your costs, maximize your revenues and get the most out of your portfolios. We will show you how to invest your money to have a safe portfolio but yet very well-performing. These techniques beat out 90% of very well-paid Wall Street brokers.

The Principles Of Highly Successful Nonprofits

What makes a Nonprofit Successful

There are key Principles to ensure success with nonprofits. This book is ideal for those that understand and work in nonprofits and also for those that intend to work with a nonprofit. Understanding these principles is paramount to achieving strong results. This book explains what good governance is and why it is crucial. These principles should be followed by all nonprofits but surprisingly only a handful of them do follow these principles. This is what divides the successful from the struggling nonprofit.

The Definitive Chief Financial Officer

How to Succeed as a CFO and a finance Manager

This book is a must-read for anyone looking to move up the ranks in the finance field. It is essential for CFOs to improve their leadership skills and their effectiveness. Learn what areas to focus on and which areas not to. This book explains the working relationships between the CFO, CEO and the Board. Find tips to work without a CFO while your company is growing and also find out when you need one.

GET IN TOUCH WITH THE AUTHOR

For any feedback - Please go to the following address:

https://markgruner.com/contact-us/feedback/

To subscribe with us - Please go to the following address:

https://markgruner.com/contact-us/subscribe/

For a FREE book including an advance chapter from the next book in this series - Please go to the following address:

https://greenbridgeco.com/freeinvestingguide/

ABOUT THE AUTHOR

Mark Gruner

Mark Gruner is a professional financial accountant and adviser.
He has worked throughout much
of the World with international

organizations. He has worked as Chief Financial
Officer and most recently as Director of Finance.
Mark studied at McGill University first doing an
undergraduate degree in Science in Biochemistry.
He later moved into the field of business and
did his graduate degree in Public Accounting at
McGill University in Montreal, Canada. After that,
he went on and wrote the Chartered Accounting
exam and became a Chartered Accountant.

You can find out more at https://www.markgru-
ner.com